The Sky Belongs to All

AF076471

Nilima Sinha

© **Nilima Sinha 2023**

All rights reserved

All rights reserved by author. No part of this publication may be reproduced, stored in a retrieval system or transmitted in any form or by any means, electronic, mechanical, photocopying, recording or otherwise, without the prior permission of the author.

Although every precaution has been taken to verify the accuracy of the information contained herein, the author and publisher assume no responsibility for any errors or omissions. No liability is assumed for damages that may result from the use of information contained within.

First Published in February 2023

ISBN: 978-93-5628-055-7

BLUEROSE PUBLISHERS
www.BlueRoseONE.com
info@bluerosepublishers.com
+91 8882 898 898

Cover Design:
Purva

Typographic Design:
Hemlata

Distributed by: BlueRose, Amazon, Flipkart

Contents

Part 1: Ramu 1

  Chapter 1: The Shukla Family 2

  Chapter 2: Ramu's Early Life 6

  Chapter 3: Stepping Out 13

  Chapter 4: Mrs. Mishra 25

  Chapter 5: The New Home 30

  Chapter 6: The Return Home 37

  Chapter 7: Mrs. Mishra Faces a Problem 43

  Chapter 8: Beyond Expectation 48

  Chapter 9: The Family in Chicago 54

  Chapter 10: A New Life 61

  Chapter 11: Ramu Has Run Away! 68

Part II: Sandeep Shukla 70

  Chapter 12: Sandeep at College 71

  Chapter 13: An Indian Festival 75

  Chapter 14: Sandeep Goes Home 80

  Chapter 15: The Gift 87

  Chapter 16: Speaking My Mind 92

  Chapter 17: Wedding Arrangements 99

  Chapter 18: The Wedding 105

  Chapter 19: Sandeep's Decision 114

Chapter 20: An Indian Dinner 118
Chapter 21: A Great Shock 125

Part III : Ramu and Sandeep 132

Chapter 22: Mr. Ram Lakhan Prasad 133
Chapter 23: Ramu's Story 138
Chapter 24: Sandeep's Questions 144
Chapter 25: Ramu is Ready to Fight 151
Chapter 26: Sandeep and Ursula 157
Chapter 27: Angela's Anger 163
Chapter 28: Ramu and his Daughter 170
Chapter 29: Sandeep in Chicago 175
Chapter 30: A New Arrival 182
Chapter 31: A Decision Made 187
Chapter 32: Dinner Invitation 193
Chapter 33: Ramu and his Worry 199
Chapter 34: Best Indian Hotel 205
Chapter 35: The Meeting 212
Chapter 36: Mrs. Mishra and Ramu 218

Part 1: Ramu

Chapter 1

The Shukla Family

"Where is he? I cannot find him! Where has he disappeared?"

Ramu was nowhere to be seen. Gopal Shukla tramped from the bedroom above to the kitchen below, back into the sitting room and to the street outside their home, but could find no trace of Ramu.

Gopal had woken up late. The party the previous evening had lasted a little longer than planned. It had turned convivial towards the end, with the men enjoying their drinks and the wives exchanging spicy bits of gossip with each other. However, he had been determined to wake up at the usual time the next morning and had told Ramu so. "Tea at 6.30 sharp, as usual! I don't want to be late for office," he had warned.

The tea did not arrive and it was almost eight by the time Gopal woke up. He was shocked to see the time and knew he would be late for office now. It would be a miracle indeed if he caught the eight o'clock train to the city center where his office as an investment banker was situated. Why didn't Ramua bring his bed tea on time? Careless servant - who had no idea of time and punctuality, having just recently arrived from India, where such things did not really matter.

Fuming inside, he turned to his wife Nimisha who still snored without any care beside him. No doubt she had abandoned all responsibility for fetching him the morning tea, knowing that there was someone now to look after her husband's needs. She could well afford to wake up later, since her office times were different and more convenient than his. And as for their school-going young son, Samir, it was vacation time and he could not be expected to get up early, having shut his eyes late at night after continuing to play games on his computer.

"Nimi, wake up, dear. Ramua has not come as yet. I am getting late," Gopal nudged his wife awake.

"Uh-huh, leave me alone," muttered Nimisha, "Go see yourself. Let me be."

There was nothing to be done, but to go down once again and shout for Ramua. The master of the house grumbled loudly as he reluctantly went to the ground floor. He stood near the steps leading to the basement where the boy slept, and yelled angrily, "Ramua! Ramua!" hoping that he had returned now from wherever he had been.

There was no answer. Was he ill, perhaps? Gopal forced himself to step down further into the basement, muttering and issuing dire threats to the lazy servant who had perhaps overslept, or was taking too long in the toilet. He was surprised to notice that the door of the room was wide open. Stepping in, he found the bed empty and the sheets gone. The worn-out suitcase where his clothes were stored was not there either. And finally, to his shock, he discovered that the door leading to the back garden was also ajar. Where was that idiot of a fellow? What was he doing outside when he well knew that morning was the busiest time in the Shukla household? It was his job to give his masters the morning tea, serve them a quick breakfast and see them off to their workplaces before he could relax, once they were all out of the house.

A hurried tour of the garden revealed it to be empty of all human presence. Rushing back to the basement, tramping upstairs and into the kitchen, and searching the rooms on the ground floor did not bring the lad into view either. Up the stairs once again to the bedrooms was as fruitless. With growing alarm Gopal at last roused the entire household, shouting wildly, "He is not anywhere in the house! Where has he disappeared?"

"Who, Ramua, isn't he downstairs?" wailed Nimisha in a shocked voice.

"Disappeared? Ramua! What d'you mean, Dad?" yelled Samir, rubbing his eyes unbelievingly as he ran out of his room.

"Must be around. Don't be such an alarmist. Where can he go? He does not know anyone here in Chicago and, anyway, cannot speak English. He may have gone for a breath of fresh air outside," reasoned Nimisha. Wide-awake by now, she turned to baby Sandeep's crib and bent to change his diaper.

"Very careless of him if he has done so. This is no time to go for a walk. Well, I must leave now. Late already, as it is!" grumbled Gopal. He knew he could not afford to wait for his tea any longer, and rushed to the bathroom to shave and have a quick shower.

"Go, dear. I must leave soon, too...," began Nimisha, and then she remembered, "Oh, and what about Sam...Samir...? Who will escort him to his maths coaching?"

"I can manage! You need not come with me," Samir, who liked to show he was old enough to take care of himself, hastened to tell her.

"No, no! How can you go alone? Oh, what a mess! What shall we do?" cried his mother, ringing her hands.

The absence of Ramu left the family in a complete mess. Nimisha was forced to stay at home to look after her two kids; Gopal was late for office and the baby, Sandeep, neglected in all the confusion, wailed loudly.

Such was the importance of Ramu in the Shukla household based in Chicago, US, its members having become used to a quintessential servant back from their own country, India.

Ramu

Chapter 2

Ramu's Early Life

He had always lived with them, though Ramu well knew that his dreams were far too distant to ever turn into reality. He considered them to be just harmless bits of fantasy, based on glimpses of the glamorous life he had sometimes encountered through TV and other media.

Ram Lakhan was a decent enough name given to him by his parents, but friends, relatives and the villagers had reduced it to Ramu, or Ramua, as people in that part of the country were wont to do. The sixteen year old had not studied beyond middle school, as the high school was in another village much further off. Besides, his father needed help to farm their tiny plot and derive an income, however small, from its produce. The cow, the hens, and the crop the older man grew were just about enough to sustain his family of wife, two sons and a daughter. Ramu shared his father's heavy workload without complaining, though he would return, whenever free, to his dreams of a more ideal existence.

It was the cow that finally changed the boy's life. If it had not been for her, realized Ramu, he would have frittered away his years in Mahuatand, a remote village on the fringes of a Naxal infested jungle in Jharkhand. It was Ramu's job to take the cow, Ganga, to graze in the forest. Every morning he walked her there and returned home to help his father in the fields. Before sundown he was back in the forest to escort her home, making sure that the frisky young cow did not stray into forbidden territory.

Ramu woke up late that day, as yesterday had been particularly back-breaking. He could hear the cow mooing in the courtyard. With a sigh, he flung off the tattered sheet that barely covered his body, and jumped down onto the cold mud floor. He felt the urge in his stomach and knew it was time to leave for the fields. Soon he was back from his ablutions and ready to take up his daily chores. He tended to the cow, milked her, and then ran to fetch water from the pond outside the village. By now the sun was well above the horizon and the village was awake and bustling. It was time now to set off with Ganga. This was the best part of the day for him, for he enjoyed the early morning breeze as he walked jauntily behind her, humming the filmy songs he had heard and enjoyed.

The dew on the cabbage plants outside their hut shone like diamonds sprinkled on the velvety green of the leaves. The boy noted with pleasure the growing size of the vegetable, almost ready to be plucked and sold in the market. Satisfied, he walked past the cabbage plot, down the narrow village lane bordered with mud huts to the mango grove beyond. The lane narrowed further as he rounded a bend and tall trees began to loom close, hiding the sun's rays. Shrubs and bushes were scattered among rocks that intruded on the path as it thread its winding way into the forest. He had trod its dusty surface often and knew which route led towards the grassy patch where he could leave Ganga to graze in peace.

Soon Ramu was back at home to work with his father in the fields. Yes, their vegetable crop was almost ready to be sold. They had planted the cabbage early that year with the hope that it could be marketed much before other farmers had even done their sowing. With good care it would be ready before the vegetable became cheap in the market. This way the cabbage, as an out of season crop, was sure to fetch a higher price.

Father and son worked together on the precious crop the rest of the morning. Once they had eaten their frugal meal, brought to them by Ramu's mother, his father began to look tired. The hot sun soon made him feel so drowsy that he could not continue any longer. He retired to have a short nap. Ramu continued with the hoeing and the weeding until it was time to bring Ganga back from the forest.

Once more the boy set off down the village lane. It was early evening and the villagers were returning home from their fields. Women with pots of water balanced on waists or on heads walked gracefully by. Others herded their goats and cattle back from the forest.

Ramu admired the paintings done on the walls of the mud huts as he passed by them. It was just a few days before the festival of Sohrai, celebrated at harvest time by the villagers, and the women had worked out beautiful designs on their walls. He stopped to examine closely a bright one that caught his attention. It was an intricate design with graceful curving lines showing leaves, birds, twining stems and lotuses. In the midst of all these, stood a lone tiger. The maroon, white and black colors stood out boldly against the pale, dull brown of the mud- smeared wall.

"Do you like it?" he swung around to hear the question. It was Urmi, one of the villagers he had often seen in the neighborhood – a young girl about his own age, with large luminous eyes and a warm smile.

"Yes, I do," he wanted to reply but shyness tied his tongue and he stood staring at her and looking awkward.

"I did it!" claimed the girl with a proud toss of her head. "My mother is sick, so I did it all by myself. Pretty, isn't it?"

Ramu nodded, still tongue-tied. He gazed admiringly instead at the slender body wrapped tightly in her faded red sari. "Yes, yes," somehow he managed to mumble, "It is beautiful."

"That's better!" replied the girl, "Why don't you open your mouth and say so?" She gave him a mischievous smile that succeeded in melting away his shyness. Soon they were chatting away as if they were old friends.

"You know, you can become a famous artist one day, that is, if your work gets known in the city. I have heard about artists making pots of money," he told her.

"Hah! A villager like me! Who will make me famous?" laughed Urmi, uproariously, as if it was a big joke.

"So what if you are one? Can't a villager be an artist? Wait and see. I will make you famous one day," he answered.

"You?" She asked, unbelievingly.

"Yes, why not?" he boasted, "I am going to be rich and famous one day myself and then I shall help make you famous, too," he added.

They chatted for a while, until he remembered with a start, "Oh, I must go, or Ganga may create some mischief."

"Ganga? Who is she?" asked the girl with narrowed eyes and a suspicious glance at him.

"Our cow, what did you imagine? A girl? Of course not!" he laughed, "If I do not stay close, Ganga will go and destroy someone's precious crop."

Ramu quickly made his way to the spot where he had left the cow. Ganga, however, had not deigned to wait for him. Instead, she had ambled back to the village, taking a route that she found much more exciting. Not finding her at the spot, he hastened back, only to see her happily munching the valuable cabbage plants they had worked so diligently on.

"Hat, hat! Bhaag! Go away!" Ramu cried in panic, "Shoo!" he flailed his arms wildly at the destructive cow. She trampled across the vegetable plot, destroying more plants as she fled. Ramu chased her in and out through the once neat rows of plants and she scampered around, crushing the crop further in her confusion.

At last the boy was able to catch her and lead her out of the field and back to her usual place in the courtyard. With a loud sigh of relief, he went back to survey the damage. "Oh no, it is all gone!" he cried, wringing his hands in desperation, "What is to be done now? Babuji will be so angry. He is sure to beat me when he sees this." There was nothing to be done, however, except to wait for his father to return from the village haat where he had gone to sell, buy and chat with his friends.

Ramu's mother was fortunately inside their hut and had not seen the damaged crop. Minu, his sister, ran out on hearing the noises outside. "Arre, Bhaiya, what happened? What has Ganga done? She has eaten up all our cabbage!"

"Shut up! She has not. Look, there are plenty of plants still standing," Ramu defended himself and the cow.

Their younger brother, Sonu, soon joined Minu. He raced around the plot, shouting, "Hai-hai! Look at what he has done! Allowed Ganga to destroy everything. Wait till Babuji sees this!"

The three siblings waited for their father to return, filled with breathless excitement mixed with fear and anxiety. As the family had feared, Babuji took out his disappointment and frustration at the loss of his crop not on the cow but on his careless son. Ramu, who had never before experienced such anger, cowered before his furious father as he thrashed him with the laathi he used for support. The elders of the village came running to protect the boy from the fierce beating. His mother, too, tried her best to shield her son, but it was no use.

Ramu's body ached with the punishment he had received. But it was the loss of his dignity- that too before his siblings and the village elders- that mattered the most to him, and was just impossible to forget. He felt he could not show his face before his younger brother and sister any longer. Word of his humiliation would soon spread around the village and the villagers, too, were sure to make fun of him. And, most importantly, what face would he show to Urmi, his newfound friend? His mind in a turmoil, he could not sleep that night. By dawn he had decided. No, there was nothing to be done except to leave the place where such humiliation had been publicly heaped on him. It was better to go somewhere far away where there was none to laugh at him. He was determined not to return, even if his family begged him to do so.

As dawn broke and before the village woke up, he tied his clothes in a bundle and dipped his hand into the box where his mother had hidden the few coins she had saved. He tiptoed silently out of the house, careful not to disturb Sonu who slept next to him. Limping in pain, he slunk through the lane and, avoiding the few villagers on their way to the fields, crept towards the highway to catch a bus.

And that is how a cow dramatically changed the life of a boy who, though he had lived in a remote village in Jharkhand, had dared to dream of distant skies filled with dazzling stars.

Chapter 3

Stepping Out

For a moment the runaway boy hesitated. It was not so easy to leave the family he loved so dearly, the village where he had spent so many happy moments, and even the father whom he respected so much for the way he had struggled to look after the family. He remembered his mother's cooking, his sister's teasing and his fights with his younger brother. Urmi's twinkling eyes swept all other images off his mind and the memory of her amused laughter brought him a twinge of regret. "I will return some day, and take her back with me to make her a famous artist," he told himself as he set his shoulders determinedly firm and walked on.

Ramu stepped on to the first bus that trundled close. It was going to Ranchi, he learnt. Fortunately, he had enough money to pay for the ticket, which he quickly did. The bus was full of passengers, but he managed to find a seat next to a man in a dhoti and kurta, with a briefcase by his side. As soon as he sat down, the man turned to him. "Are you going to Ranchi? To your home or to school?" he asked, flashing his red paan -stained teeth in a smile.

"To Ranchi. I am looking for a job," replied Ramu.

"Finished your studies?" the man wished to know more.

It was on the tip of the boy's tongue to retort, "How does it matter to you?" But he held back the rude reply and said instead, "I don't want to study. Told you I am looking for a job."

"It is not that easy to find a job," remarked the man, "You should have finished your studies first."

Ramu ignored the advice and turned his face away. The man caught the hint and did not talk any more. Instead, he began to doze and was soon deep in sleep. Relieved, the truant lad stared at the world outside the speeding bus. It was the first time he had travelled so far away from home, he thought, letting his eyes feast on the green hills and the 'saal' forests that rushed past. The road cut through brown rocks as it made its way through the coal belt. Then the bus slowed down as it drove carefully up the 'ghaati'. The road twisted and turned, steep walls on one side, the other falling into a deep valley.

Ramu's stomach soon began to grumble and growl, reminding him that he had not eaten anything at all that morning. He felt desperately hungry. Job or no job, he had to eat, he decided.

A little later, fortunately for the hungry boy, the bus stopped near a row of shops, in the midst of which was a 'dhaba' where passengers could refresh themselves. Forgetting everything else, Ramu jumped out.

He glanced at the name of the place, put up on a board above the 'dhaba'. "Lovely Palace Hotel" it proclaimed in bold, black letters on a pink background. He hurriedly followed the passengers to a makeshift hall furnished with crude benches and tables, occupied by bus and truck drivers, their helpers, and laborers on their way to construction sites in the city. A fire blazed in a brick chulha in a corner, presided over by a fat, mustachioed cook. Ramu rushed straight to the man and blurted out, "Can I have something to eat?" The cook looked at him in surprise, and pointed to a table, "Of course! But go and sit there. You will be served food at that table. What do you want?"

"Anything. I am starving," he replied.

The man nodded and led the boy to a table. "Here! Eat." A plate of rice and daal, with a little heap of mashed brinjal was set before him. Ramu devoured the food hungrily and licked his hands clean.

"Satisfied? You were really hungry, it seems," he heard and looked up. It was the man he had sat next to in the bus. In his rush to grab something to eat, he had not noticed that he had also decided to eat there. Ramu nodded and, feeling better now, smiled at the man. "Did not eat this morning," he explained.

"Thirty rupees for the meal, sir," he heard, and turned around to see. The man standing beside his chair had extended his hand towards him.

"You have to pay for that meal, dear boy," the bus passenger reminded him with a smile.

"Oh. Yes, of course. How much?" asked Ramu.

"Thirty, sir," repeated the waiter.

"Thirty? But I only have ten left!" exclaimed Ramu, dismayed.

The man, impatient now, glanced angrily at him. "Why did you come here then? Didn't you know you have to pay? I will have to inform the 'maalik'," he threatened before he strode off.

Ramu glanced around in panic. He must quickly run away, before the waiter returned with the hotel owner. But the man at his table had his eyes fixed sharply on him. "No need to fear, boy. Weren't you looking for a job? Offer to work here. They always need extra hands. I am sure he will be happy to employ you," he suggested helpfully, "You'll be alright. Wish you luck!" With a friendly pat on the boy's back, his companion strode out to join the other bus passengers.

He was right, realized Ramu. Why not work there? It was as good a place as any, and he would never have to go hungry at least, with all the food being served at the 'dhaba'.

The owner turned out to be sympathetic to his predicament and agreed to employ the boy. Ramu heaved a sigh of relief. His forgot his pain in his excitement at having secured a job so easily and so soon.

How different was his life now! All around him he could see the bright lights of the highway 'dhaba'. There was a constant movement of traffic that rushed past; the honking of buses and trucks rang loud in his ears, as did the chatter of customers enjoying their meals. The noise and clatter of the busy place prevented his thoughts from wandering back to the past that he had left behind so impetuously. Yet he missed the old life at times – the delightful hours spent under the open sky, the long walks under the trees to take the cow to the grazing grounds, and the very satisfying feeling of watching plants, tended lovingly by Babuji and him, grow in their little plot of land.

There was no time to think of the past, however, for it was work all day for the boy. That night, too, it was late as usual. The crowd of travellers had at last been taken care of. "Now to bed!" sighed Ramu, "I am so sleepy". It was a relief to throw himself down to the floor in the room that served as a store for the 'dhaba'. He was about to fall asleep when, "Hey, you, boy!" came the voice of the mustachioed cook, Gopal, "Come out! There is more work for you!"

"Oh no, so late?" grumbled Ramu. He walked out of the store with reluctant steps. A group of men in uniform sat around the table in the far corner. "Here, take it to that table!" ordered the cook, thrusting a tray at him, "Dinner for those policemen. They have turned up again today, and just think, at midnight! But they are big people; we must look after them, however late it may be!"

Gopal informed Ramu that policemen from the local patrolling party came there often to have dinner, never bothering to pay for it. The 'dhaba' owner, eager to please the important guests, did not dare to ask for payment. Instead, the staff was instructed to serve them with all due courtesy. So, with a sigh, Ramu did as he was told and began to look after the eminent diners, running back and forth to bring them the hot 'chappatties' they had ordered.

Suddenly, the peace was shattered by the sound of a sharp gunshot. A group of men he had not noticed before sprang out from a dark corner of the room. The policemen, sitting relaxed at the table, enjoying their meal, immediately jumped to their feet and reached for their rifles. But before they could do so the attackers, their faces hidden under masks, had overpowered them.

Shocked, shaking with fear, Ramu ran and hid behind the wooden door at the back. He heard the noises and the scuffle and dared to peep out. The policemen were still surrounded by the attackers. But one daring policeman had managed to break free. In a flash, before he could be caught, he had picked up his rifle. He raised his arm to fire. Just then, a shot from another weapon rang out. The next moment the policeman collapsed in a heap on the floor, dead. Ramu gasped in horror at sight of the blood dripping from the man's neck, for he had never seen anyone shot before.

Everything happened fast after that. The attackers gathered up the policemen's rifles, and ran out of the room. He heard the revving of motorcycles and in a few moments they had all vanished from the scene. The policemen, free from their clutches, raced out to catch the culprits, but the attackers had already escaped into the darkness.

All that followed was a blur of confusion for the lad. He learnt that the men who had attacked and seized the rifles of the patrolling police were Naxalites from a neighboring jungle. Officers making inquiries and the police searching the premises now invaded the hotel. "Come on, tell us. Did you know those men?" Questions were thrown at the boy. "I d...d...don't know," Ramu mumbled his answers again and again, but the policemen persisted with their inquiries. He was questioned several times, though he kept proclaiming his innocence. Some officers, even more aggressive, slapped him and shouted at him to confess.

Confess what, Ramu had no idea. He crouched, frightened and trembling, before the uniformed men towering over him, hoping they would soon go away and leave him in peace.

Life became normal and peaceful only after several days had passed. But Ramu was no longer happy with his job at the 'dhaba'. It was not just the shock of the Naxalite attack; it was the nerve-racking questioning, the probing, and the inquiries - when he had no secrets to reveal - that was so disturbing. Who knew when another such incident might happen again? Who knew when he would be thrown into jail, for something he was ignorant about? The fear continued to haunt the boy.

No, this was not what he had bargained for when he had decided to leave home. The ever- demanding crowds, the clanking of dishes and the noise and the smoke inside the 'dhaba' irritated him. If only he could be back in the peace and tranquility of the sun washed fields at home, he thought. He now remembered with pleasure the whisper of the leaves as they swung in the morning breeze when he walked to the forest, and even the mooing of the cow that had caused the destruction of the crop. The cleaning of dirty dishes, the fetching and carrying of trays and the sweeping of filthy floors was not a job he wanted to continue any longer.

There was no other alternative, however. So, though his heart was no longer in it, the boy continued to perform the monotonous tasks, dutifully, mechanically. The owner soon noticed his lackadaisical attitude. Once or twice he warned him about it. "Pay attention and learn fast. Or....!" He did not say more, but the words were warning enough.

Ramu decided he had had enough. He had to leave, look for something better.

The truck driver was quite a regular to the place. He was a kind hearted person, always pleasant and not in as much of a hurry as the others. The boy rushed eagerly to serve him every time he came. The man had given him a good tip the first time he had set the 'thaali' before him, and continued to be liberal with his tips. Surely he is a good man, and will help me if I ask him to, thought Ramu. After the truck driver had finished his meal, he requested him to come outside for a moment. As soon as they were out of earshot of the other 'dhaba' employees Ramu spoke to the man, in a low voice, "I don't want to work here anymore. Do you know where I can find a better job?" he asked hopefully.

The truck driver looked surprised. "Why? Don't you like it here?"

"No. I am tired of all the washing and the running around! Also, I feel scared. Those policemen, and all that firing! Suppose it happens again? Please, find some other work for me! I want to go away from here," begged the boy.

The man nodded and looked thoughtful. "I will try," he said, returning to his truck. Ramu waited eagerly for the driver to return. A few weeks later, he was back at the 'dhaba'. He smiled at Ramu and whispered to him to come outside. "I have something for you, Ram Lakhan."

Ramu liked the man for addressing him by his full name, and not the short one that others used. Greatly excited, he followed him out of the restaurant.

The driver told him his truck had been hired a few days ago to transfer a family's belongings from Patna to Delhi, where the family was shifting. After it had been unloaded at the new home in Delhi, the 'memsahib' in the family asked him if he knew anyone who could help her with household chores in her new home. She had even offered to pay him a commission if he could find her a 'boy' from some village to work for her.

"I immediately thought of you! It is better than wearing your feet out at this dirty, crowded place. What do you think?" the driver asked.

Ramu was silent for a few moments, wondering if working in a home would be any better than doing the same at a 'dhaba'.

"I will give you a small part of the commission if you agree. You are bound to get better pay there. I have heard that it is very difficult to find a servant in a big city like Delhi. Servants are in great demand there, you see." Noticing the doubt on his face, the driver tried to convince Ramu.

Servant? Ramu felt offended, shocked. He was a farmer's son, heir to a plot of land, however small, he was not about to lose his respectability by being called someone's servant, a slave, no less.

The next moment frightening images of the last few days shadowed his eyes. It would be good to escape to another place, to forget what had happened. Not just this, there was the lure of the big city, that too Delhi, the capital from where the whole nation was ruled. The two thoughts were strong enough to negate all his doubts.

"What does the memsahib's husband do? Is he a big shot 'sarkari' boss?" he asked innocently, eagerly.

"Oh yes. You know they are all rich and important people in Delhi. They live in big houses, have parties, watch TV all day and have a grand life. You are sure to like it – it is so different from your poverty stricken existence in the jungle here," explained the truck driver, Shyamu.

"Oh... that is just what I wanted!" Ramu agreed happily, impressed by the description of city life.

The 'dhaba' boss was reluctant to let him go. "What is this? I gave you a good job, fed you well even when you neglected your work – and now you want to leave? This will not do. I will cut your wages if you go. And what about the plates you broke? You will have to pay for them!"

When the boy stubbornly stuck to his decision to leave, he could do nothing except to deduct a large amount from the wages due to him. Ramu had no option but to accept the meager balance amount. He meekly agreed, and left with just a few paltry rupees - but with a lot of hope.

The big city! Delhi! A huge step forward! He climbed eagerly into the truck, clutching his little bundle of clothes, and was soon on his way to a new life.

The truck driver drove at a furious pace, honking hard whenever he saw an obstacle on the way. He slowed down only when they passed a crowded bazaar or met goats or cattle crossing the highway at their own leisurely speed. Some of the bigger cities had bypasses through which they could drive fast, but in the majority of the smaller towns the route led through residential as well as market areas. Ramu enjoyed driving through the bazaars, catching glimpses of the various goods that were displayed in the shops. Their flashy colors and variety fascinated him and he wondered when he could acquire some of it for himself.

The truck driver, Shyamu, was a talkative fellow, sometimes chatting only to keep himself from dozing off. He gave the village boy much needed advice about the job he was about to take up in Delhi. "Remember, humility is a much valued quality in an employee. No master would like his staff to talk back. Just say, 'yes sir' or 'yes madam' and then carry out whatever task you are assigned. Eat whatever you are given, even if it is old or stale, and in the utensils assigned for the use of the staff. Do not use the glasses, spoons or plates in which your master eats. Do not sit on a chair before your master. Remain humble and obedient. That way you will please them and they will learn to trust you. And once they have begun to trust, you can afford to relax a little. They will not mind even if you contradict them sometimes," he laughed, "Once they have begun to depend on you, you will see they will be literally eating out of your hands. But remember, it will take time. You must be patient...," and so on, until Ramu stopped listening and let his mind wander off.

He was alert once again as the truck neared their destination. Shyamu parked the truck near a dhaba on the outskirts of the city and told the owner, a friend, to look after it. "We cannot drive the truck there," he explained to Ramu. He hired an auto rickshaw instead to reach the home of Ramu's new employer.

As they drove on, Ramu stared, wide-eyed, at the roads and fly-overs, the shiny cars, the well-dressed crowds, the fashionable shops with the decorated, brightly lit windows and the trees and gardens of the great city he had only dreamt about.

This was life; this was his dream come true, the place where a great future awaited him. He felt he had arrived.

The Mishras

Chapter 4

Mrs. Mishra

"Ma'am, there is a man at the gate. He wants to meet you."

"Who is it? I told you not to disturb me," said Mrs. Mishra, irritated. She had been reading, and had just reached the point when the young man in the book was about to confess his love to the girl. Reluctantly, she put the book down and looked up. "Alright, find out what he wants," she ordered.

"His name is Shyam. Says you know him," replied the peon who had brought the message to her.

Mrs. Mishra sighed. She put the book aside, and heaved herself up from her comfortable couch. She followed the peon down the corridor and out to the front verandah. Before her was a man who looked vaguely familiar. Her eyes were drawn to another figure, just behind the man, whom she had not noticed before. She glanced suspiciously at him - a lanky, scruffy boy with a thick untidy crop of hair, in clothes that looked as if they had never been washed. Who was he? Was he begging for something, she wondered? She glanced again at the burly man who was pushing the boy forward. She looked inquiringly at him and back at the dirty stranger.

"Madam, you seem to have forgotten. You had asked me to find a boy in the village who could come and work for you," the older man reminded the forgetful lady.

"Oh, yes, I had. Now I know. You are Shyamu, right? So you've found someone? Good. I have still not been able to get anyone suitable. Is this the boy?" she exclaimed, examining the youth from head to toe, staring at him till he began to fidget uncomfortably. "Well, he looks a poor villager, no doubt. Is he fresh from there? Has he worked before? What is your name, boy?"

"His name is Ram Lakhan," Shyamu informed her, "He has come to the city for the first time. Has no experience, but will learn."

"Ram Lakhan - that is too grand a name for a 'chhokra'!" Mrs. Mishra made a face, and declared firmly, "I shall call him Ramu."

"Ji, madam, as you wish," said Shyamu respectfully, "You wanted a boy straight from the village, with none of the airs or demands of someone who has worked in Delhi, so I brought him for you. He is from Jharkhand and has never worked in a household before."

"Achha. How old are you, boy? Can't he speak?"

Ramu mumbled something that she failed to hear.

"Speak up. Have you been to school? Can you read and write?"

"Yes. Studied till Class 8," Ramu spoke with more confidence.

"What? Well, I did not want to have someone so educated. I don't have that kind of work. Sweeping, cleaning floor, washing utensils... that is all he would do. Class 3 would have been sufficient. He will start demanding more after a time, and I won't have that," she protested.

Shyamu hastened to assure her that the boy was humble enough and without any airs. "Class 8 means nothing, madam, you know how they teach in village schools. He is ready for any kind of work, however menial, at whatever salary you are willing to pay. And above all, he is still an unspoilt, innocent, village lad, someone you may trust."

"Alright, if you say so. How much does he expect? He looks absolutely untrained. I will have to waste a lot of time teaching him," Mrs. Mishra reminded the two sternly.

After some haggling, during which Ramu stayed tactfully silent, the pay was fixed at Rs. 3,000 a month, along with food and a corner to stay, no fixed hours of work and no specific work allotted. "He is not to refuse anything he is asked to do, must be ready for everything. I am a good mistress, will treat him well. But he must be obedient too."

And so it was all fixed. She watched as the boy followed the driver to the gate to bid him farewell, ignorant about the fact that it was actually to take his share of the promised commission. She waited for him in the verandah, and noted the satisfied smile on the boy's face as he returned. So he was happy with the salary, which she well knew was too low for all the work she had in mind for him. But, she shrugged, he was new after all, and would have to be trained.

Mr. Mishra was a senior officer in the government, privileged to stay in an exclusive Lutyens bungalow with a huge compound and six rooms specifically meant for the staff. Of course Ramu was just a boy, she thought, who did not need the luxury of living in one of the quarters meant for the more senior household staff. In any case they were already occupied. The driver, the cook, the two peons, the gardener, and even a tailor had been allotted the six rooms. A corner of the verandah in front of the kitchen would suffice for the boy, she decided. She led him to the space allotted, showed him around, and told him he could stay there. "Here, take this soap and wash yourself well. You look really filthy. I certainly don't want infections to be brought into the house."

The lad looked happy enough as he settled down in the corner she had shown him, she was relieved to see. She had feared that he would demand a room too, after seeing the homes of the other staff in the compound. But he seemed satisfied with the space she had allotted him in the bungalow. Good. He would be available all twenty-four hours. She could call him even at odd times in case she needed him, unlike the other staff that retired to their quarters when free. She watched apprehensively as he put his grimy bag against the wall, pulled out some shabby clothes from inside and glanced questioningly at her.

"Yes, yes, you may bathe under that tap outside. The gardener uses it to water the plants near the kitchen, but you are free to use it, too. And there's that toilet next to the tap. It is also meant for the staff. You may go there!" she offered.

The boy nodded shyly. He waited for further instructions, but impatient now to return to the novel she was reading, Mrs. Mishra strode off, leaving him to stand there uncertainly.

Ramu

Chapter 5

The New Home

"Go on, go, take a bath and clean yourself! Didn't you hear what Madam said?" An elderly man, stepping out from the kitchen, addressed the boy. Ramu turned around and saw him for the first time. Obviously he was someone who worked for his new masters.

"I cook for Sir and Madam," explained the man. "They are good people. But you will have to work hard, if you want to please them. Where are you from?"

"From near Ranchi, in Jharkhand," mumbled Ramu.

"Oh, from the jungles? Yes, I have heard that the area is all jungle. Never mind. You will soon learn the ways of the big city. Now go and bathe."

Feeling cool and fresh after his bath, Ramu returned to his corner. He wondered what he must do next. The cook nodded to acknowledge his presence but seemed too busy to give him his attention. Nervous, Ramu just stood and stared around at the room. So this was how a rich man's kitchen looked! How clean and gleaming! He stared in wonder at the counter with the gas stove, the pair of sinks with a tap each, one for the clean, and the other for the dirty dishes, the shelves lined with gleaming crockery and the neat cupboards; all so unlike the dirty 'dhaba' he had been working in earlier.

"You can go outside if you like. Or rest there in your corner. Madam will call you when she is free," advised the cook.

With hesitant steps, Ramu walked out into the garden. How neat and beautiful it was! The green lawns stretched till the gate where the sentries stood, there were graveled paths leading to the house and to the staff rooms at the back, trim hedges, and colorful flowerbeds lining the lawns. So unlike the wild forests around his village! And what a contrast to the 'dhaba' beside the busy highway! It felt as if he had entered the grounds of some king's palace, he thought with awe.

"Hey, you!" someone called out to the boy, as he roamed about in the garden. "You cannot just walk here! Go to the quarters at the back, or go do your work in the house! You have not been employed to wander around!"

As the boy learnt later, the man who ordered him back into the house was the driver, who turned out to be a friendly person. The curt order made him whirl quickly around and retreat to his corner near the kitchen.

"Madam wants to speak to you; she is in the back verandah. Come, I will take you there," said the cook when he saw him. The man led him into the house, through the pantry and the dining room, and into the informal family room at the back. It was a well-lighted, carpeted room with colorful curtains, drawn aside to reveal the trim lawns in the back garden. Here, too, there were neat beds filled with pretty flowers. A mango tree stood in the centre of the lawns. A peacock, flaunting its colorful plume, strutted about on the grass. Ramu watched the bird, fascinated.

"So, have you settled down?" he heard and turned his gaze away from the scene outside. Madam was sitting comfortably on a sofa in the room. She had finished her book, and was now ready to give her attention to the servant she had just hired.

But Ramu was now gazing with admiration at the furnishings, the decorations and the luxuries inside the room. He had seen such stuff only in the TV movies he had seen sometimes. How fortunate he was to view it now with his own eyes!

Mrs. Mishra smiled to see the dazed expression on the boy's face. "Like it? Very different from your home, isn't it?" He nodded silently, feeling awkward before his new employer.

"You will have to learn a lot," she warned him.

It was the beginning of the training that Ramu was given. His way of working had been so different, he realized. In fact, he had to learn his job all over again. He did not know that floors had to be wiped with a mop on a handle, and utensils washed not by crouching on the floor under the tap, but by standing before the sink in the kitchen. A picture flitted across his mind – his mother squatting on the floor surrounded by blackened pots and pans, rubbing them vigorously with ash and a handful of dry grass. He had done the same at the dhaba where he had worked.

No crouching on the floor any more, swiping the floor with a wet rag, he thought with relief. Instead, he now stood tall and proud, wielding a rod around with a flourish, while the mop at its end did its job of wiping the floor clean.

Working in the big city was something to be enjoyed for its novelty, rather than the drudgery it was at his earlier workplace, he concluded happily.

It took the boy almost a month to become adept at all the dusting, sweeping, cleaning, washing and wiping that needed to be done in the bungalow. But he loved the hours spent in the various rooms of the grand house, admiring the beautiful objects that they contained. Why were there so many rooms for just two people, filled with things they hardly ever used? Another bit of luxury? Because the two could shift from one room to another, if they got bored with the first, he concluded finally.

Every object in the house was a marvel to Ramu. So that was how the rich lived, he thought, every time he witnessed something new. Filled with curiosity, he felt awed at the opportunity to glimpse the lives of the privileged. He performed his chores diligently and picked up the new ways fast, to the satisfaction of his employers. Before too many days had passed, he was serving at the table, carrying tea trays smartly when visitors came and washing the precious crockery carefully enough not to break any.

A few months later he had graduated as an all-rounder servant, who could sweep, clean, wash, do household shopping and even iron clothes washed at home. And when the cook left on a month's leave, he was enlisted to do the cooking too, which he had picked up while assisting the old cook.

"You are doing well, boy. I am happy to see that you are a quick learner," Ramu was thrilled to hear. It was a few months later. Mrs. Mishra had called him to the family room where she usually relaxed, once her husband left for his office. She smiled and handed the boy a package. "See, I have got this for you, as a reward for being a good worker."

Surprised and curious, Ramu took the package from her and fingered it hesitantly. "Go on, open it," she ordered.

It was a set of new clothes; he saw with delight. Eagerly, Ramu unfolded it to find a brand new pair of trousers and a shirt with blue stripes! She had made the tailor, who lived in the staff quarters, stitch the clothes specially for him, Mrs. Mishra informed Ramu. He accepted the trouser and shirt gratefully.

"Go on, put them on," she ordered, "You may go to the tailor's room to change. I am sure he must be eager to see how it fits."

Ramu rushed to change into his new dress. The tailor informed him that he had observed him closely each time he visited the area and was glad to see that he had assessed his size correctly. "Yes, it fits well!" agreed Ramu, and walked to the big mirror that stood there. How smart he looked, he thought, as he preened himself before the tall mirror. Just like any other youth in the big city! No longer did he look an uncouth village boy.

"Ask Madam to give you leave for the day. You have been working so hard. Surely you deserve some time off. I don't think you have seen the city yet," suggested the tailor.

"Will she let me go?" asked the boy hesitatingly.

"Why not? You have not taken any leave since you came," replied the man.

To Ramu's great joy, he was granted leave for a day. The driver, friendly now, advised him to take a bus that would take him towards India Gate. He even led him to the bus stop and helped him get into the right bus. Excited, Ramu sat down, to look out of the window and enjoy the ride. He had a good view of the city as they drove through the wide, tree-lined streets of New Delhi, passing the grand old buildings on the ridge from where all the important, great, 'sarkari' people, ruled the country. He also gazed with respect at the dome that rose in the middle of the buildings. That was where the highest of the 'sarkari rulers', Rashtrapati ji, resided.

Getting dropped, he walked down the Central Vista towards the tall, impressive India Gate, taking in the sights of the smart, well-dressed young men and women who strolled on the manicured lawns.

Balloon sellers, ice-cream vendors and chana sellers had parked themselves on the sidewalks. Ramu joined the crowd near the ice-cream cart after checking his pockets to see if he had the money. There was enough, he saw with satisfaction. Licking the cool, sweet, strawberry ice cream with delight, he sighed with satisfaction.

He had done it! He had made it to the big city, and could now enjoy all the wonderful things that were available there.

At last, as the sky began to darken, he decided to return to the bungalow that was now home to him. Asking for directions, walking rather than taking a bus, he reached late at night, exhausted but happy. Sahib and Madam had retired to bed by then, and the staff had returned to their rooms at the back. He dropped down on the durrie that served as his bed and was immediately asleep.

It was work all day again from next morning, but the boy did not mind.

A year later, when Ramu, who had at last begun to miss home and family, asked for leave to visit his village, Mrs. Mishra readily granted him his wish. "Just fifteen days, if you do not return on time I will cut your salary," she warned him sternly. Happily he wished her goodbye and set off for home.

This time, instead of the shabby bag he had arrived with, there was a shiny suitcase in Ramu's hand, filled with the gifts that he had been able to buy for his loved ones.

Chapter 6

The Return Home

Ramu was bursting with excitement as he stepped down from the bus at the very stop he had stood on as a runaway from his home two years ago. Well, he had made good and returned not only with money in his pocket, but gifts for his family, too. How surprised his father would be when he handed him the crisp notes he had earned. And the gifts – sari for his mother, bangles for his sister and a T-shirt with Delhi written on it for his brother – were bound to bring smiles on their faces. He quickly patted the other secret gift he had brought, a pair of pretty little silver earrings for someone else whom he had not forgotten. Urmi, of course!

His arrival created the expected stir in the village. Crowds gathered around the prodigal son, proud that one of them was not only working in far off Delhi, but earning a regular salary too, according to the few letters sent home by him. Back home, he was greeted with happy tears from his mother. His father caught him in a warm embrace. "But you should not have left without telling us, beta! We were so worried. And your mother cried her eyes out, waiting to hear from you. You didn't even think of her feelings," he reproached his son.

Minu and Sonu clung to their brother and complained as well. "We missed you, bhaiya. Why did you go away?"

That evening, Ramu's mother cooked his favourite 'dal-bhaat bhujia' for him. After the celebrations for his homecoming were over, Ramu pulled out the precious envelope from his pocket. "Babuji, this is for you," he said softly as he handed over the packet to him.

"What is it, beta?" Babuji fumbled as he opened the envelope.

The whole family crowded around to watch. There were loud gasps as the crisp new notes came into view. "So much?" his mother breathed out at last.

Babuji just looked at his son with eyes that were brimming over with tears. "Arre beta, all this earned by you? Must be thousands of rupees!" he said in an awed, trembling voice.

"Just a few thousand," said Ramu modestly, "I do not have to pay for my home and food. I have a place to sleep and enough to eat, given by my 'maliks'. I did not waste my pay. I saved it all instead! "

"Bless you, beta, bless you, ble..e..ss you!" Babuji's voice broke into sobs. Ramu could not help the moisture from rising in his own eyes as he bent to touch his father's feet. His mother embraced him quickly before he could reach her feet.

The cow incident had obviously been forgotten long ago. Their boy had brought back valuable cash that definitely amounted to more than what the cabbage crop would have fetched. All was forgiven, forgotten, as the family welcomed their son back. That night, Ramu stole out to the courtyard to give Ganga a pat on her back.

"It is because of you that I left. I am not angry with you anymore. In fact I am grateful, 'meri pyari Ganga'!" he muttered softly in her ears. The cow gave a gentle 'moo' in answer.

The stipulated period of leave was soon over. The days had flown by only too fast, with Ramu and his friends and family savoring every moment of every day spent together. The highlight of the visit was, of course, his meeting with Urmi once again. "You promised to make my art famous," she reminded him with a pert smile, "What are you doing about it"

"I will, some day," Ramu repeated the promise he had made, this time with greater confidence. He pulled out the special gift he had bought for her out of his pocket and presented it to her with a flourish.

"What is this?" she asked in surprise.

"For you, brought from Delhi!" mumbled Ramu, shyly. He watched her face eagerly as she opened the box. The expression on her face, of excitement, followed by joy, was a delight to watch. "Put it on," he urged.

She did, and lowered her eyelashes modestly. "How does it look?"

"You look beautiful," he murmured.

The visit was soon over. Ramu returned to Delhi and work, dreaming of coming back again the next year with even better gifts and larger savings.

The next two years passed more or less the same way. As he bid goodbye to his family after his third visit his mother accosted him.

"You have worked hard, beta, and made our lives so much easier and comfortable. Your father was getting old and now because of you he need not work so hard in the fields. I was wondering. Isn't it time you brought home a daughter-in-law?" she asked.

The image of a laughing face appeared before Ramu's eyes. "Yes, yes, Ma. All in good time. Maybe next year when I come…". He left the sentence vague, not promising anything, but the sentence made him think.

It was time, perhaps, to approach Urmi with a serious proposal and a firmer commitment. Suddenly it struck him. How was it, that, unlike several other girls in the village she had still remained unmarried? Of course it was fortunate for him that she was still not wedded, but was she perhaps already promised to someone? The thought made his heart beat faster in a mixture of dread and something he could not quite define. It was this that made him rush to meet the girl. He saw her as she walked back to the village from the pond where she had gone to fetch the water. A brass pot was balanced on her head while another was clutched at the waist. Her hips swaying gracefully, she ambled down the village lane, a smile lighting up her face as her eyes fell on him.

"So? Time for you to leave?" she asked.

"Yes. Tomorrow morning. I will catch the bus early in the day," he replied.

"And when do you return? As usual, a year later?"

"If you wish, I can do so earlier also," Ramu offered.

"How? What do you mean?"

The question made Ramu blurt out boldly, "Tell me, is your family thinking of getting you married? Are you engaged?"

Her answer delighted him. "Oh no! I have told them I wish to do something, not get married like all other girls in our village. And know what? I have joined the girls' high school in the next village and walk there every day! My parents pester me from time to time, but I made them promise they would not take any step before asking me...."

"And they agreed?"

"They had to. I can be very stubborn, you know. I want to study, go to college... maybe become a famous Sohrai artist. And don't forget, you promised you'd help me!" though she said it with her usual impish smile, Ramu could see the hope shining in her eyes.

"Yes, I did. Wait for me then!" he told her with a strange flutter deep inside him.

"I will," she answered, her voice now low and shy. Their eyes met and he could feel her response to feelings he had hardly expressed. He knew, however, that she felt the same as he did and a warm glow of happiness lightened his heart.

She would wait for him; he was sure of it. She would resist all other offers and even her parents' pressure as she waited for him to return once more from the city. The contented glow continued to warm his heart as he caught the bus to Ranchi once again. No long truck drives awaited him. He had already purchased his return train ticket, days before he had left for his annual leave in the village.

The Mishras

Chapter 7

Mrs. Mishra Faces a Problem

Mrs. Mishra felt satisfied – she had trained her servant well. No more did she need to supervise the boy nor did she any longer need to give him his orders. He seemed to know instinctively what was required of him and how he could keep his master and his wife pleased. The old cook had retired by now, as expected, and she now trusted Ramu and was dependent on him for all the family's domestic needs.

Ramu did not know it, but Mrs. Mishra had realised that she had found a good servant, willing to work twenty-four hours if needed, and do whatever she wanted him to, without any objection, unlike others. In fact she had decided already.

Ramu would replace the cook who had left. There was no need to look for anyone else, she decided. The boy could already cook the normal, everyday dishes, and she now planned to teach him the special Bihari dishes she had learnt from her mother as a young girl.

During festivals the family liked to savour the traditional Bihari delicacies enjoyed in childhood. The old cook, who had been trained in the North and had worked with families with sophisticated Western tastes was too arrogant and looked down on the rural preferences of the Bihari officer he was employed by.

Ramua, on the other hand, was eager to please and a quick learner. Mrs. Mishra began to teach the boy the special dishes she had learnt from her mother, like 'pedakia' filled with nuts and 'khoya', the 'pua', and 'thekua', besides the more mundane but just as tasty 'litti chokha', 'daal bhari poori, 'chane ka saag' and 'bachka'. Various types of chutneys and pickles made up the rest of the list.

Ramu had no idea that it was all planned deliberately. He enjoyed learning the new dishes and when some morsels were given to him to taste, he ate them with relish, grateful for the offering.

Fortunately Mrs. Mishra had enough time to train the boy, as her husband led a very regular and predictable life. He left for his office at North Block at exactly the same time every morning. Some days he took his lunch with him, other days when his schedule was not so heavy, he made a short trip home to have his lunch and doze off for a while. Back to office again, to return home only in time for dinner. Evenings he watched TV and on weekends played Bridge with friends at the Delhi Gymkhana, or went golfing, followed by lunch with his cronies at the Golf club.

Mrs. Mishra herself was more active. She loved to go shopping. And then there were her kitty parties thrice a week in the various groups she had joined, and occasional visits to her close relatives (of which there were many, Delhi being a busy metropolitan city where people from all parts of the country tended to congregate because of the availability of jobs).

Into this peaceful, ordered existence suddenly burst a disturbing bombshell, bringing unwanted change into her life. Mr. Mishra suddenly fell sick. She rushed him to hospital where it was discovered that he had had a massive heart attack. Mrs. Mishra hastened to inform her only child, daughter Nimisha, who lived in Chicago with her husband, Gopal, and family.

"I am coming, Mamma," Nimisha quickly decided, "You are all alone there. Who will take care of the two of you?"

"No, no! How can you do that? You have Samir and Sandeep to look after. Samir's school would be open too," Mrs. Mishra protested. Deep in her heart, however, she felt relieved to learn that Nimisha was ready to take over the responsibility of caring for her father. So what if I do not have a son, she thought proudly, my daughter is more capable and responsible than any son could ever be.

"Oh, we will manage, don't you worry. Gopal can look after Sam and I will bring the baby," Nimisha insisted.

Just two days later Nimisha Shukla arrived from Chicago. She soon assumed control, sitting by her father's bedside, administering his medicines and accompanying him to the hospital, leaving her mother to take care of baby Sandeep. Between trips to the hospital and receiving the relatives who descended on the family to sympathise, the days passed with scarcely any time to rest.

To Mrs. Mishra's relief and joy her husband recovered soon. Doctors, however, advised a major heart surgery, as all his three arteries were choked. And it had to be done fairly soon. "An operation?" cried Nimisha, dismayed. "How will you manage alone, Ma?"

"I am sure there will be people to help us. Don't worry. We will manage somehow."

Nimisha continued to worry about her father. "I am sorry I cannot stay on to help you, Ma. There is my work, and Samir's school, and..." she said, feeling miserable about leaving her parents. Then it struck her. "Oh, but how about you coming to Chicago for the operation? That way we would be able to take care of you, and the doctors there are as great ... Gopal, too has good contacts. He can have it all arranged. Yes. That is the best solution. You must come to the US so that we can look after you."

Mrs. Mishra shook her head. "No, no, it will be too much trouble for you, dear."

Nimisha, however, insisted, and was backed by husband Gopal who rang up the Mishras and added to the pressure.

At last Nimisha's parents succumbed to their daughter's pleas and agreed to accept the invitation.

Mrs. Mishra, however, continued to worry about the additional burden she was imposing on her daughter and son-in-law. "You will need help to take care of the invalid," she said, "You won't be able to manage the two kids, your job, and the two of us - one a patient- on top of everything. I will be there to help, of course, but…," she shrugged with an air of helplessness.

"I do have someone to work, Mamma. She comes once a week. And I have put Sandy at the baby care, so it is not such a problem," Nimisha hurried to explain.

Mrs. Mishra continued to feel guilty about giving so much trouble to her daughter. How could they make life inconvenient for Gopal? No, no, a traditional, respectable family like hers would never impose itself on a son-in-law.

She fretted and worried until at last she had an idea. She raised her finger and said in a triumphant voice, "I know! Let's take Ramu along. He will be of great help. He can do the cooking and the running around while we concentrate on hospital and the nursing, without having to neglect the kids. You will be able to continue with office and work and there will be no problem."

Nimisha looked doubtful. "Mamma, you do not understand. It is not easy to get a visa. Who will give him one? You know Americans are very particular about granting visas. Forget it."

"Oh, we will get the passport and the visa made. Do not worry about it. We know the right people!" Mrs. Mishra assured her confidently.

The issue was discussed in detail and plans made. The Mishra family would take Ramu along with them to look after the patient, not only while they travelled to Chicago, but also later while he recuperated from his operation.

Ramu, however, had to be informed and his consent taken before they could proceed with their plans. Would he agree?

Ramu

Chapter 8

Beyond Expectation

"What? You want me to go to Amrika?" asked Ramu, gaping at his mistress in shock and disbelief.

Of course he was greatly excited when he learnt of the plan to take him to America. From a remote village to the country's capital, and now across the seven seas to the great land he had heard so much about, what a mighty leap it would be! He had never imagined, in all his fanciful dreams that this too could happen one day. The exciting news left him dazed. It was something he could never ever have anticipated, no, not in his wildest thoughts. He blinked back unbelievingly at Mrs. Mishra.

"Yes. Will you? We need you there. Do not worry - it should all be over in three months time," explained the mistress, wondering if he would agree and hoping with all her heart he would not refuse.

The first excitement was soon replaced by other thoughts in the servant's mind. "I... I don't know," Ramu mumbled, now doubtful. His thoughts had flown back to his mother's question about his marriage, leading naturally to his conversation with Urmi.

"What d'you mean - you don't know? Anybody else would jump at the idea! Going to America is the dream of everyone I have met, and here you say you don't know! That is the most absurd thing I have heard. Come on, inform your people and send them money, or do whatever you need to. And prepare yourself for the journey," ordered Mrs. Mishra, deciding to exercise her authority over the servant.

But Ramu was now silent, a troubled expression on his face. He felt confused and in two minds. The temptation to accompany the Mishra family was indeed great, but then so were his feelings towards the girl who had come to occupy a significant place in his heart. A furious debate arose within him. He spent a restless night wondering how he could resolve his predicament. Perhaps he could marry her and take her along. Surely she would be welcome as an extra hand in the American family. She could well pursue her painting hobby also there. Would his formidable mistress agree to the additional cost of taking another pair of hands not necessarily required?

It was Nimisha who removed his doubts and made Ramu feel better. "Come on, it is not such a big deal," she tried to persuade the reluctant servant, "You can return the moment Dad is a little better. Can't you spare just three months for your sir and madam who have looked after you so well? Specially when Dad is sick?"

Ramu stayed thoughtful and silent. No doubt it was true that good days had come to him ever since he had started to work at Delhi. His pay had increased by another thousand, he had learnt several skills, not just cooking and cleaning, but - he smiled a secret smile - driving, too! While Mrs. Mishra rested in the afternoons, he had quietly joined a driving class in the neighborhood, and in three years managed to procure a driving licence, that too an international one. It was quite an achievement. He was proud of it. Some day, he would graduate to become a driver, which was much more respectable than being known as a servant. Not just this, his family back in the village had been able to build another room at home. And now Babuji was saving to pay off the loan he had taken several years ago when his mother had fallen seriously ill and had to be rushed to a hospital at Ranchi. He weighed the pros and cons of leaving the job and returning to the village, to Urmi and his family, as opposed to flying away to America to an unknown future.

But before Ramu could decide, Nimisha confronted him once again.

"Come on, stop wondering...it is not the end of the world. You can always return if you do not like it and as I said, it is not for always...it is just for three months and perhaps even less if Dad is able to return before. And let me tell you what I have suggested to Mamma...we will raise your salary to Rs. twenty thousand a month if you come. Think...in three months you would have collected a good amount. More than half a lakh, in fact!"

At first he could not believe it. How? After some calculations done with paper and pencil when alone, Ramu's eyes widened in amazement. Nimisha Ma'am was right. In fact it would be more than the amount mentioned by her. Well, he must reconsider the offer, or was it the 'order', in which case he must obey, being a dutiful servant, after all. It would not be so difficult; not returning home for three months was not such a calamity.

Thus did Ramu convince himself that it would only be to his benefit if he agreed to go with the Mishra family to the 'phoren' land. Once he had made up his mind and informed Mrs. Mishra events moved fast. Mr. and Mrs. Mishra tapped all their resources to get a passport quickly made for Ramu. The making of the visa was a difficult task but they ultimately succeeded in getting a six-month visa made as a special favour to a senior officer who was sick. Nimisha, in the meantime, arranged to meet Ramu's other needs; she bought a warm coat and a sweater for him. Some of his old T-shirts were given away and replaced by smarter shirts.

Ramu made his preparations too. He wrote two letters, the first to his family to inform them about his going, and another to Urmi to plead with her to wait for him and not to give in to her parents' pressure to marry her off.

Urmi promptly wrote back to tell him she could wait for him for eternity, what was six months to her? And he was to remember about her ambition and do something about it. Maybe America would prove a better place for developing her into a really famous artist, she hopefully added at the end.

His Babuji, too, was full of hope. "It is such a great chance, beta. Maybe you will come back a rich person with so much money we will be able to buy more land and build a two-story pucca house. And marry off Minu into a rich family!"

Dreams, dreams, thought Ramu with a wry smile. He too had dreamt of reaching the skies; maybe it was time for everyone's dreams to come true. After all, as he had heard, Amrika was a land of opportunity. Whoever went there, returned with loads of money. His spirits lifted at the thought and he began to look forward to the journey with growing excitement.

All preparations needed to leave were soon done. It was time now for the travellers to pack up their suitcases. Mrs. Mishra secured the household, with strict instructions to the staff staying in the quarters to take care of the premises, and carefully collected all necessary papers.

Soon the travellers were packed in two cars to drive to the airport.

Ramu's heart pounded in eager anticipation. He had seen planes only in the sky and never on the ground or from close. This itself would be something new for him, to get inside one and fly in it was beyond all imagination. He was soon settled into his seat inside the plane. After making sure he was comfortable, the others walked to the front to take their seats.

Everything was strange and fascinating for the first time plane traveller. As the Air India flight soared into the sky he clutched the arms of his seat in alarm, looking down at the lights that twinkled far, far below. How distant they had become! Inside, it was all cosy and warm. Beautiful girls served the passengers drinks. He shyly accepted a glass of water, feeling thrilled at the idea of someone so glamorous 'serving' him, a servant. He did not want to sleep, even when the lights went off and the co-passengers around him snored away loudly. He stared into the darkness while thoughts - of anticipation, excitement and wonder, swirled around in his mind.

Ramu remained in a daze as the plane landed, several hours later, at Chicago. Nimisha's husband, Gopal, had come to receive her and the others. As the car sped towards their home, Ramu sat at the edge of his seat, watching it all in growing excitement and amazement. He had never seen such a grand, dazzling city before, even though he had lived for three years in the capital city of Delhi. So many high buildings touching the skies, so many cars and buses, and so few people! No wonder it was so impressively clean and tidy, unlike the crowded bazaars in his country!

At last, when they drove up the driveway of the Shukla house and he saw the elegant mansion with its sloping roofs, gleaming walls and its many shining windows, his mouth fell open in admiration. He was led inside and taken to the basement where a room had been kept for him. It had its own toilet and bath, a kitchenette and glass doors that opened into a tiny green lawn, luxuries he had never experienced before.

Ramu drew in his breath and shaking his head in awe he muttered, "Where have I come? This is what heaven must be like. To think that I am lucky enough to reach it in this life itself."

The Shuklas

Chapter 9

The Family in Chicago

Nimisha's husband, Gopal, now took over the responsibility of caring for the invalid. He had already made the necessary appointments and drove the elderly Mishras to the hospital. Nimisha was left to introduce Ramu to her family, home and the work he must do.

She felt satisfied to see that the Indian help adapted himself quickly to his new surroundings. Nimisha taught him how to use the various unfamiliar gadgets, including the dishwasher, the vacuum cleaner and the washing machine. She was happy to see that her son Samir took to the new arrival immediately. Though the two could not communicate as they spoke different languages, she found that Samir enjoyed teaching Ramu. In the process, both Ramu and Samir picked up a smattering of English and Hindi.

Mr. Mishra's surgery was successful and he was back from the hospital after a week. It was now Ramu's job to attend to the recuperating gentleman, cook his special meals and run from kitchen to bedroom, carrying food and taking care of the patient. Keeping additional local help would have been so expensive, whereas he was available to them all twenty-four hours, that too, for just a few thousand rupees, which was nothing in terms of dollars.

"See, didn't I tell you he would be useful?" remarked her mother with a triumphant air.

In just about a month, Ramu became a trusted, invaluable addition to the Shukla household. It was his duty not only to look after the patient, who had almost recovered by now, but to do almost all the cooking, shopping for grocery, and also a bit of the gardening, as part of his daily routine. Looking after her son, Samir, was a duty he seemed to particularly enjoy, with Nimisha often requesting him to amuse the baby, too.

"How different he is from Rosie! She is very efficient and clean, I know. But somehow one feels more comfortable with Ramu. Why is that?" wondered Nimisha as she sat chatting with her mother over a leisurely cup of coffee one Sunday afternoon.

"Get rid of your Rosie," said Mrs. Mishra dismissively, "Ramua can clean just as well. He is used to working hard, but has nothing much to do, now that your father is so much better. Why not? Instead of sitting in his room twiddling his thumb, he may as well do the cleaning! You will save some money at least."

"And what will I do after he leaves with you? No Mamma, Rosie is a good worker. We are used to her and trust her. Who knows, I may not find anyone as good as her after you take Ramu back with you. Let him help with cooking, shopping and other tasks, but I shall not let her go. She is so good, keeps the house really shining."

"Find him something more to do, then, otherwise he will become lazy sitting around, watching TV, or playing with Samir. Cooking and shopping are not enough to keep him busy," advised Mrs. Mishra.

"Let him enjoy his stay a bit. In India he must be working like a donkey. I can imagine, with a hard taskmaster like you, he must be on his toes all twenty-four hours!" laughed Nimisha indulgently.

She was forced to rethink only a few days later. Rosie, her industrious Mexican help, informed her that she was thrilled, delighted and very happy because her boyfriend had proposed to her at last. "No more housework, you will be my most cherished wife and I will take good care of you," he had told her tenderly. The two planned immediate marriage and then they were off to a long honeymoon in Europe. "I am sorry to leave you, but you understand, isn't it?" Rosie said apologetically as a pink blush suffused her cheeks.

There was no alternative for Nimisha except to congratulate her and wish her all happiness in her new life. Mrs. Mishra was all cooperation. "Do not worry, beta. Ramu is here. He will help. Ramu!" she called out.

The servant was in the kitchen, frying Gopal's favorite pea 'bachka' for the family. It was a weekend, when everyone was at home, enjoying hot, freshly cooked 'daal-bhaat', potato 'bhujia', and chicken curry, all cooked Bihari style as only Ramu could do, with the pea 'bachka' as his special dish.

"Listen, you will have to take up the cleaning now. You know Rosie is leaving," ordered Mrs. Mishra in her most peremptory tone, which did not brook a refusal.

"Acchha, madam!"

"And not once a week only, as Rosie did. You are an in house help. We give you food as well as a luxurious room to stay in. You must work daily, and whenever needed, or ordered to. After all, there are children here. When they dirty the house, you must clean it. It will be your duty to maintain the place and keep it as neat and shining as she did."

"Theek hai, Madam," agreed Ramu meekly.

Nimisha did not really wish to spoil her son by allowing him to 'dirty' the place as her mother said. She had brought him up to throw litter in garbage cans and maintain tidy surroundings. She had struggled hard to ensure that the brat followed certain rules set by her. Not wishing however, to contradict her mother who was much too indulgent towards her grandkid, she held back the words on the tip of her tongue.

Nimisha tried hard to find a replacement for Rosie. She explored all avenues, putting up ads in the newspapers and at stores, spending time interviewing the applicants, but found it difficult to select anyone. Mrs. Mishra, who sat at interviews with her, found none of them to be suitable, when compared to those available in her home country. She found fault with all. "They are so stiff – a maid must be flexible, be ready to do anything we ask her to – she cannot dictate rules and terms! After all she is not your equal! Why, you even allow her to sit before you!" she admonished her daughter for being too kind and polite with the house workers who applied.

"It is different here, Mamma," protested Nimisha, "And please don't call them maids, they are household workers, or helps. Being termed a 'maid,' will offend them!"

Mrs. Mishra only shook her head disapprovingly. "What 'offend'! You don't call a spade by any other name, do you? Ha! Ha!" she laughed.

There was no point arguing with her. Her mother was too set in her orthodox ways of thinking, shrugged Nimisha. However, she tried to make up for it by being extra polite to Ramu for carrying out any task she burdened him with. She also reminded Sam not to be too rude while playing with him, and not to make fun of him when he made a mistake or did not understand him.

Mr. Mishra soon recovered well enough to yearn for his normal life back home. When he expressed his desire to leave just two months after his operation the doctors were confident enough to give him their approval. They assured him he was fine and there was no need for him to stay an invalid. He was well enough now to travel and get back to a normal life. His wife was happy to hear this. It was great to be with her daughter but she had already begun to miss her friends, her kitty parties and her activities at Delhi. Nimisha tried to persuade her parents to remain longer there, but the elderly couple was eager now to resume its own pursuits. As the day of departure drew closer, Nimisha doubled her efforts to find alternative help.

"Ramua can stay on if you want," offered her mother generously, "I am sure it will be easy for us to find another 'chhokra' in India. Who knows? He may turn out to be even better than Ramu. He has become rather spoilt working here using all those machines – washing dishes back at home by hand and doing laundry may become a chore for him now! You can send him back whenever it is convenient for you. After all, I have got him a six month visa, he is free to spend more time with you."

If Ramu had looked forward to returning before the six months were over, he would have been very disappointed indeed. But when Nimisha, who thought it better to consult him regarding his wishes, spoke to him, his answer surprised her. "No Ma'am, I am prepared to wait. After all, what are six months in a man's life?"

"Hey, but what about your marriage plans? I thought you were eager to return home?"

"I will be able to save more if I stay on. I know 'badi memsahib' is sure to reduce my salary again once we are back. Since I am earning more here, I am happy to continue in your service. I will be grateful if you allow me to serve your family, at least for a few more months," pleaded Ramu humbly. He had already calculated that six months would mean one lakh and twenty thousand rupees! Back in Delhi he would never earn such a sum in such a short time. He could do so much with that amount, including a grand wedding with Urmi, he thought.

Well, he was right, thought Nimisha. From his point of view, it would definitely benefit him monetarily to stay on. It was a relief for her, too. Imagine, having a help who would be available all twenty-four hours! Not just this, he would not make a fuss if she loaded him with additional duties. It was a luxury never available with local helps, and that too, at a much lower cost.

Ramu

Chapter 10

A New Life

And so Ramu stayed on, while his employer, Mrs. Mishra, along with her husband, returned to India.

How glad he was to learn that he could continue working in the new country! It was so different here, Ramu realized, even from Delhi, where he had lived after leaving the 'jungles' of Jharkhand. Yes, the old cook in Delhi was right. His village home was just the 'wilds' to him now, after he had experienced the wonders of the big, wide world.

No doubt about it. He definitely enjoyed his new life in a country he had never imagined he would ever set foot on. His thoughts flew to Urmi. Oh, how he longed to see those bright, laughing eyes once again. Then he remembered and consoled himself. Her last letter to him was reassuring, for she had promised that she would wait for him. It was only a matter of a few months and they would be together again, forever. And in the meanwhile, he was making more money here than he would have done back home.

Not just this, the new family was definitely more considerate to him than his masters back in Delhi. Though a servant, he was treated here with greater dignity. And why not? He had watched Rosie, the girl who came every week to do the cleaning, work there silently and efficiently. No one interrupted her, nor ordered her around. She did nothing extra, only what she was hired to do. True, she did it all very efficiently, but no one disturbed her while she worked. She was not suddenly ordered to make tea or "Bring that here, will you?" or "Do this, or do that!" nor was she yelled at to carry out other random tasks.

In short, she was just another respected human being. She was certainly not a lowly, humble slave to be ordered around and to be kept in her place, under the masters' feet.

When he had seen her the first time, Ramu had mistaken Rosie for an American guest visiting the family. Nimisha introduced them to each other. Rosie, he remembered, had smiled and politely shaken hands with him. It was only when she picked up the vacuum cleaner and started to work that he realized who she was.

How scandalized he was one day when he saw her make herself a cup of coffee! Not only this, she then sat down calmly on a chair at the central table in the kitchen. How could she, a servant like him, dare sit down and have coffee? What would her mistress say? But no one said anything. It was accepted as normal, whereas, if he had done the same, Madam would certainly have been wild at him.

Now that his Madam had returned to Delhi, he was not expected to be available all twenty-four hours. Nimisha was not as demanding. He had his fixed hours of work, and could retire to his comfortable room in the basement when off-duty. The small TV kept there for his use added to his joy.

The relationship between master and 'help' here was so different here, he thought. Working in the Shukla household in America was real pleasure, much more than it was in Delhi. Ramu loved operating the dishwasher and the washing machine; he enjoyed learning new English words, as well as playing exciting computer games with Samir. Looking after the baby was fun, too.

Yes, he felt appreciated here for the work he did. Nimisha was certainly more polite and considerate; she requested, rather than shout out orders. And those words – 'please' and 'thank you'- often used by her, made him feel even more special.

Ramu enjoyed his trips to the neighborhood grocery store to pick up exotic stuff he had never seen before. Then, one day, Nimisha took him by train to the Indian store downtown, from where she bought the spices needed for the Indian food they ate more often now. Ramu loved the train trip to the city. The sights and sounds of a place so very different from anything he had seen before were so exciting, so eye-opening!

Ah, and the Indian store! He remembered it with pleasure. The next time he went there alone, now confident enough to travel by train to the city.

The owner – cum – salesman greeted him with a cheerful 'namaste'. He helped him choose the spices he needed to buy and then, speaking Hindi with an unfamiliar accent, asked him how long he had been in the USA.

"About three months," answered Ramu, in his own different accent.

"A new arrival! And how do you like it?" the man seemed to be in a chatty mood.

"Bahut accha! So different from our 'desh'!" said Ramu, smiling at the man, delighted to meet someone else from his home country.

"You will be staying long?"

"No. I am here only for a few months. I must return soon."

"And why is that? Don't you like it here?"

"I do, but...!" Glad to meet someone friendly he could be free with Ramu blurted out the whole story.

The man nodded his head and asked once again, "Are you happy here?"

"I am....but," Ramu's mind went back to his village, his family, and Urmi.

"You can stay on, if you like," the man told him, to his surprise.

"Stay? How?"

"And earn more than you have ever done," added the salesman, his eyes closely watching Ramu's face.

"I earn well here. Five times the amount they give me in Delhi," said the boy, beaming a proud smile.

"Uh huh, you have no idea what you can get here!" laughed the man. With some probing he was able to find out the exact amount received by Ramu. "Is that all? They are fooling you," he told him.

Ramu did not reply, but the man's words left him feeling restless and disturbed. He would be returning soon, he told himself, for his stay was only to be for six months. He must be grateful to the Shukla family for paying his fare both ways and bringing him here, if only for a short period. It was an experience he would treasure all his life, for after all otherwise there would have been no chance of his travelling and seeing a wonderful, new and different life. And finally, in any case he himself had no desire to extend the stay any longer, for he was committed to returning home to family, wedding, and Urmi.

A nagging dissatisfaction, however, continued to erode his peace of mind, urging him to find out more. The next time he went to the Indian store he drew the salesman aside and asked him, "What kind of job, bhai?"

"Aha, feel tempted, is it? Well, there are many. You could be a cook in an Indian restaurant – that is, if you can cook Indian dishes, or, if you drive you may run a taxi, or... Oh, there are many alternatives. Provided, of course, you leave the present job... So, how about it?"

"Madam has taught me many dishes. They like what I cook. Bihari food, mainly. But I think I am not bad at other stuff, too. Like, normal everyday cooking, and kebabs and kormas...," Ramu replied confidently.

"Bihari? That sounds great. I don't think there is any such restaurant here. Maybe, with so many of them settled here it could draw good crowds. If you like, I will try to find out. Give me some time".

The man looked up with a broad smile as soon as Ramu entered his shop a few weeks later. "Hey, I have been waiting for you! I have a good offer for you, if you are interested in taking up another job."

Ramu's eyes widened with curiosity. "Another job? What do you mean?"

"Look, call me Raman. Let us be friends, first of all. I know someone; he is also from Bihar. He was so excited to learn that you are a good cook. He asked me to find out if you would like to join him in running a restaurant where they would serve authentic, rustic, regional food from - 'Purabia' was the word he used. I am not familiar with the area, since I come from far away, that is, the West. I mean, Gujarat. Our cuisine is very different."

When Ramu remained silent and thoughtful Raman gave him a sharp glance.

"So?" he asked.

"What will he give me?" Confused and uncertain, Ramu questioned the man at last.

"Something you would not have dreamed of, a share in the profit, in addition to a monthly income of four hundred dollars. It depends on how well you do. If you succeed in drawing in a good clientele ... well then, the sky is the limit!" smiled the man.

"But.... but what about my, what do they call it, visa? It is only for six months," reminded Ramu.

"Oh, that? It does not matter. There are many others like you, living here without the papers. It can be managed, don't you worry," said the shopkeeper airily, dismissing his doubts.

"It is too sudden for me, let me think about it," muttered Ramu. He quickly collected the spices he had come to buy, and walked to the tram station. It was bright and sunny outside. It was the fall season and the trees were colored in all shades of brown, orange and red. He had never seen such a beautiful world before, not even in the forests he had lived next to and he let his eyes absorb it all in wonder and appreciation.

What would it be like to live here forever? The thought struck him and he was forced to give it his attention. Well, why not? Maybe it was time now for his dreams to come true at last. He could always send for Urmi and live happily here forever and ever with her. What a life he could give her, and she was sure to find great opportunities here for her artistic ambitions to grow into reality.

For a few days Ramu continued to waver. Was it right to leave the family that had brought him here? They had been good to him and he had no complaints about the way he had been treated, specially since he had arrived in the new land. His Delhi madam had made him work hard, no doubt, but she had also taught him useful skills.

But then that offer – of being a partner in a business rather than just attending on a family as a 'servant', or 'help', as termed here, was just too tempting. Part owner! A big step up the ladder to reach the stars he had always dreamt of! No, no, he could not miss the opportunity - he decided at last.

The Shuklas

Chapter 11

Ramu Has Run Away!

At first, Gopal and Nimisha could not believe that their quiet, meek and obedient servant could have dared to step out of the security of their home into an unfamiliar and strange world. He was sure to return, even if he had been tempted to step forth to savour a new life for a while. He had made a mistake in leaving his comfort zone for the great, wide, unknown world beyond its walls. They waited, confident that he would soon return. As the days passed and there were no signs of Ramu coming back their worries increased, making them anxious and angry.

"Maybe we should have informed the police," said Gopal a few days later.

"Let us search his room thoroughly. He may have left some information behind about where he planned to go. Let us find out," suggested Nimisha.

They searched the basement room as well as the rest of the house but failed to find any clues about the missing servant.

Mrs. Mishra was furious when she was informed that Ramu, the boy she had trained with such effort, had suddenly vanished from her daughter's home. But she had already found another 'chhokra' in India and was busy training him just as she had trained Ramu, and therefore, did not think about it any more.

Gradually life returned to an even keel once again. Nimisha doubled her efforts to find another help and soon succeeded in finding one.

The family did not get any news about Ramu. They made inquiries from friends and acquaintances, in case anyone had seen him anywhere, but could not discover the slightest trace of the once loyal servant. After a time the Shuklas gave up.

Soon, Ramu became a forgotten chapter in the life of the Mishra and Shukla families, both in Delhi and in Chicago.

As days passed into months and then into years the Shuklas forgot that anyone like Ramu had ever entered their lives. He no longer existed in their memories.

Time flew, as it always does when one is busy bringing up a family. The years go by as fast as the turning wheels of an express train and before one realizes it, the children are grown up, first into difficult teens, and then into bright young individuals.

And so it was with the Shukla family.

Part II: Sandeep Shukla

Chapter 12

Sandeep at College

The coffee shop at the University campus was crowded with young people chatting noisily as they sipped their coffee and munched their snacks. Sandeep, hungry as always after his vigorous game of tennis, looked around for space to put down his tray of brownie, chips, and coffee.

"Hey, no place? Come and join us!" he heard and looked up gratefully. A group of cheerful faces smiled welcomingly at him.

"Thanks, guys. Glad to sit down. Have had a tough match. The other chap really pushed me around. My legs are aching with all the running around I did on the court," explained Sandeep. He wiped the sweat off his forehead and plunked himself down on the one empty chair.

"We can see that. You do look tired. Make yourself comfortable," said a girl. She turned to her companion, "So? What did you tell him?" she asked, resuming her animated conversation with her companions and forgetting the new arrival.

Sandeep was too busy himself to bother about the talk around him. He picked up the brownie and bit greedily into it, enjoying the crisp, and at the same time juicy, chocolaty first bite as his teeth sank into it. The chips too were crisp and hot. As he washed it all down with the strong, hot coffee he felt rejuvenated once again, enough to attend to what was happening around him. The friendly group was winding up, ready to leave.

"Goodbye. Enjoy! Meet you some time," said the girl who had first spoken to him. He really saw her this time. She was tall and slender with a smooth, olive skin and long, raven black hair. And yes, she was attractive, with a pert nose and full lips that were slightly open now, revealing white, sparkling teeth. Not bad, he thought, as he watched her walk gracefully out of the room.

It was Sandeep Shukla's final year at New York State University where he had been admitted after finishing school in Chicago. He had grown into a tall, handsome boy with an athletic body and a crop of thick black hair. Both he and his elder brother Samir were now based at New York, where Samir was now working in a Bank while Sandeep was still at college. Nimisha and Gopal's younger son had got a room in the dorm where he stayed with another boy, Ben Maddock, from the South. The two got along well enough, though the roommate stayed up late into the night, playing games on his computer and greatly disturbing Sandeep who liked to sleep early. He had protested at first but the boy said he could not sleep and needed to occupy himself with some entertainment, so he better put up with him somehow if he did not want his roommate to go totally insane. Sandeep had bought himself an eye pad, and cotton wool to block his ears, and tried his best to catch some sleep. Fortunately he had become immune to the disturbance by now and paid his companion back by snoring noisily throughout the night.

Sandeep enjoyed his life at college. Besides classes, he took interest in games such as tennis and basketball, and participated enthusiastically in social activities such as debating and theatre. Not only this, because of his friendly nature and readiness to participate in various college activities he became a popular young man. He was also good at organizing events and mobilizing youth to get together for meetings and college functions. It was at one of the social events organized by him to protest against gender and other forms of discrimination that he met the girl again.

"Hi! Haven't we met before?" she asked, settling herself on the sofa next to him. She screwed up her eyes, trying to remember where they had met. Sandeep smiled; he knew it well.

"Uh..hh..hh. Have we?" he asked, pretending not to remember.

"I am sure we have. But....where?"

"Your face certainly looks familiar. Are you studying here?"

"First year. Social science. And you?"

"Final year. History!"

There was no time for more. The speakers, Sandeep among them, were requested to step onto the stage. "Excuse me. Hope to see you again sometime," he said as he walked up to take his seat. When his turn came he spoke confidently against gender discrimination and on the need to give equal treatment to females in jobs. "Their roles are as important and significant as us males'. There is no reason why they should end up as secretaries and assistants. Why can they not be our CEOs and Chief Managers?" he ended as cheers broke out amongst the girls in the audience. Several of them rushed to shake his hand as he finished his speech and stepped down from the stage.

"Great!" exclaimed a familiar voice as his eyes met those of the girl he had spoken to earlier. "Appreciate your views. Hope you really mean it?" she laughed, "Or are you saying it only to win us females over to your side?"

"Why? Don't you believe me?" asked Sandeep.

"Well, hope you get a chance some day to prove it!" laughed the girl.

"If I ever am in a position to do so!" Sandeep laughed it off but in his heart he wondered if such a situation would ever occur in his life.

"I am sure you will be. By the way, I am Ursula. And you?"

"Sandeep Shukla. But you did not tell me your second name. What is it?"

"Ursula Pershad," replied the girl.

"Are you of Indian origin?" wondered Sandeep,

"Guess!" teased the girl, "I must go now. See you sometime!"

Puzzled and mystified, Sandeep could only stare at her receding back as she swung around gracefully and walked towards the exit.

Chapter 13

An Indian Festival

There was an air of festivity in the gardens adjacent to the dorms at the university campus. Lighted paper lanterns hung from poles and strings of coloured bulbs swung from pillar to pillar. On the steps and along the verandahs were neat lines of small earthen lamps filled with oil, little cotton wicks aflame in them, reminding some students of Diwali celebrations back home in India. Indian music streamed loudly from loudspeakers, lending a cheerful atmosphere to the scene.

The students gathered there were in high spirits. A big group of boys and girls squatted on a mat spread out in the verandah, cards in hand, playing 'flush', traditionally enjoyed during Diwali. And in the open space in front of the building young men and women played around with 'anars' that sprouted fountains of sparkling stars up into the air, 'phuljharies' that sprayed bright sparks of light when lit, and 'aatishbaajis' that soared high into the sky leaving behind them trails of light and sparkle – all various kinds of fireworks bought from the Indian store downtown.

The table, towards which the students flocked from time to time, was loaded with a range of mouth-watering, fragrant sweets and spicy savories. Sandeep, as one of the organizers of the event, smiled with satisfaction, happy to watch his friends and colleagues enjoying themselves. Blacks, browns and whites, girls and boys - all mingled together freely and happily to celebrate the festival symbolising the return of the ancient Hindu king, Ram to his capital city Ayodhya, after vanquishing Ravana of Lanka, who had kidnapped his wife Sita.

A group of chattering girls, like a flock of birds, descended on the scene. Clad in their colorful festive dresses, they immediately attracted the attention of all the male students present. Heads turned, activities were put on hold. Who were they? Juniors, from first year, guessed many, as they saw familiar faces encountered before. It took Sandeep a few seconds to recognize the girl he had met earlier– Ursula Pershad. He greeted her eagerly, "Hi! Come and join us!"

"Oh, can we? I have brought my friends to show them how Diwali is celebrated!"

"Welcome!" called out many voices. Soon the newcomers had become a part of the happy group. The students enjoyed the celebrations; some playing cards, others bursting firecrackers or lighting sparklers, and still others just binging on the eats and the drinks. The merry chatter and the laughter of the young people enjoying the festival lasted far into the night. At last, tired and sleepy, the boys and girls left for their rooms and dormitories, to dream away the few hours left for the arrival of a new day.

Sandeep remembered the celebrations with delight. He had come a little closer to Ursula, who had chatted freely with him of this and that. They had had a great time lighting the sparklers together and when tired of it, playing cards where she had won many rounds and made quite a neat sum for herself.

"This calls for a treat!" he had whispered in her ear.

"Why not? Will you have coffee with me tomorrow?" she had laughed.

"Sure! I will!" he had replied.

And now here they were, just the two of them, sitting cosily together in the very café where they had first met.

"So? How are you?" he asked, suddenly feeling shy.

"It was great fun last night," she answered in her usual chatty way, "I am glad we went. My friends were curious. They wanted to be a part of the fun…. So I said, let's go. I am sure those guys won't mind our joining them…. And so we all dressed up and took a chance….I'm so glad you welcomed us!"

"Naturally we would. Who wouldn't? We were so happy to see all the pretty girls landing there so unexpectedly!"

"And the girls also enjoyed the fun and the eats!" she told him.

"Thanks. Glad you did. It was I who organized the whole thing. With a few of my friends," Sandeep could not help boasting. After all he had worked hard, collecting funds, going to the Indian store to buy the fireworks and getting the Indian eats, finding a place for the function and inviting others to come and celebrate a festival not all would have cared about. He was proud to know that it had turned out to be a success, as the girls informed him.

"The next time you organize an Indian function, I will be happy to help you," offered Ursula, "I am not as familiar with them as you may be, but I do have some idea."

"So there is an Indian connection! How?" asked Sandeep, still curious about her, as she had not responded to his earlier question about her parentage.

"Does it matter so much? After all everyone belongs to the great melting pot that is the US. We are all Americans. But may I ask – what are you? An Indian come to study here, as so many do, or US born?" she was as inquisitive about him as he was about her.

"Guess. That's what you asked me to do about you, isn't it?" he laughed.

"Well. So who will answer first?" she smiled.

"I was the one who asked first!" he parried the question.

"Hmm. So you did. There is no mystery. I am half Indian, born here, so fully American. Now your turn!"

"Well, Indian American," replied Sandeep.

"And now that the great mystery has been solved, do have the coffee," reminded Ursula.

They chatted on for a while, lightly, in a friendly way, enjoying the coffee, along with the snacks that were

Sandeep's contribution to the get-together. The conversation gradually turned to a more serious subject.

"Did you face problems of social discrimination, being Indian and brown in a class of whites?" Ursula asked, her voice grave.

"I don't think anyone bothered, as far as I remember, during my primary school years. Later, when I went to high school, my classmates maintained a bit of a distance, but once they realized there was no difference between them and me in accent or behavior they accepted me as one of them. No, I had no problems," explained Sandeep.

There was silence as the two went back to their different childhoods and school days. "Guess you had no problems either!" said Sandeep, looking pointedly at the large green eyes that stared back at him from under thick black eyelashes. He watched as a pink blush coloured her white cheeks. Embarrassed by his steady gaze, Ursula hastily looked down at her coffee.

"N...no, not really. It is the other discrimination that makes my blood boil. I mean, gender discrimination, about which you spoke so effectively the other day, at the meeting we both attended."

"That's because I believe strongly in it," replied Sandeep, pleased with her reference to his speech.

"I must go now. I have to finish my assignment," Ursula rose to bid goodbye, "But we had a good time. Thanks."

"When do we meet again?" asked Sandeep.

"Well, I am going to be too busy the next few days to socialise!" laughed Ursula, walking off.

Chapter 14

Sandeep Goes Home

Before the two could see each other again, it was time to go home for Christmas. Elder brother Samir, well settled in his bank job at New York, took leave, too, and the two travelled home to Chicago together. It was typical Christmas weather there. The sky was dark and snow fell lightly to the ground. The trees, bereft of their leaves, stood black and bleak against a white background. Their home, however, looked cheerful and cozy, with a warm glow that greeted the two brothers as they drove up the path to the portico. The door was opened immediately for them as soon as they reached, even before they could press the bell.

"Welcome, welcome, Sam, Sandy!" Nimisha greeted the two arrivals with open arms, while Gopal beamed at them from behind her. Their mother hugged her sons enthusiastically. Gopal stepped forward and shook hands with them warmly.

"We have a surprise for you," said Nimisha, as soon as they had settled their baggage in their rooms, "Come and see... look who is here!" She led the two boys to the family room where a figure sat on the sofa by the fireside. She had white hair and a lined face but her eyes were alert and back still straight and stiff.

"Nani! Grandmother! When did you come?" shouted Samir, walking over to the old lady. He bent and respectfully touched Mrs. Mishra's feet, as he had seen other Indians do to greet their elders.

"Happy to see you, Nani. No one told us you were coming," Sandeep glanced reproachfully at his parents before following his brother's example. His grandmother blessed them and, as they straightened up again, hugged the two boys close. "No need, boys, no, no! I would rather embrace the two of you!" she cried warmly. "Bless you, dears. How you have grown, both of you," she exclaimed gushingly.

"We were not sure about her ourselves," Nimisha explained, in reply to Sandeep's accusation. "Your grandmother was alone since your grandfather passed away two years ago, as you know. I have been telling her to come and stay with us, but she always resisted. 'You know I have my own life. I will be alright', she told me every time I pleaded with her to come stay with us. But then she fell sick last month. And...."

"I thought it would be nice to go see my grandsons. I can always return, if I miss my Delhi home too much!" interrupted Mrs. Misra, smiling at the two boys. "And it is great to see you both – such fine, strapping young lads! Bless you!"

"So glad to see you again, Nani. Hope you stay on!" responded Samir, and he meant it. He remembered with pleasure the stories she used to relate to them at bedtime, and some of the delicious snacks she had cooked when she visited them years ago, when he was a little kid.

"We hope she does," added Gopal politely.

The old lady had settled down in the guest room downstairs. Having her around meant more Indian meals, noticed Sandeep. It created more work for the maid who came home to help, for grandmother was now too old to do any cooking herself. Instead, he watched with amusement as his grandmother directed their Mexican help to cook the Indian dishes they wanted to eat. The help never really came up to the senior's standards! It was fun to watch the two talk to each other about culinary procedures, accompanied by much gestures and signs, for the girl's English was not good enough to follow his grandmother's directions.

After one such interaction, he found his grandmother sitting on the sofa in the family room, holding her head in frustration, after Sara, the help had left. "Baap re! How has your mother kept her as a cook here? She does not even know the basics of cooking! It is so difficult to make her understand. What a contrast to that young boy who picked up so fast."

"Which young boy?" asked Sandeep. As far as he knew, they had always employed female helps and in any case, males hardly ever worked in homes.

"Oh, that boy...don't you remember, oh, you may not know, it was so long ago. You were just a baby then. What was his name? Ram? No...I remember now. It was Ramua! He disappeared one day...! Did you ever see him again?"

Puzzled, Sandeep remained silent but Samir was quick to reply, "Of course I remember, Nani. Ramua! He just vanished one day, I remember well! I used to play with him when I was a kid. Tried to teach him also. It used to be such fun - he could never get the American words right! I had to pronounce the new words many times before he could say them correctly. But he was good at games. I used to get so angry - for he managed to beat me several times! And then suddenly, one fine day, he just disappeared. We never saw him again. Wonder what happened to him. Strange, isn't it? How can one just vanish?"

"When one wants to one can, I suppose," said Nani thoughtfully," At first he did not want to leave India and his home, but once he experienced the charms of this country, I guess he decided to live here forever. That is why he must have run away, knowing well we would not allow him to stay on. Ungrateful chap!" She ended in a disgusted tone. "Anyway, let's not talk about that stupid servant. That ungrateful 'chhokra' doesn't deserve a mention!"

Sandeep did not care about it, one way or another, as he was lost in his own thoughts. They had been preparing for Christmas and had bought each other gifts. He had earned some money working in the library back at college and had spent it on gifts for the family. A scarf for his mother, gloves for his brother, a book for his father, chocolates for his grandmother and, finally, a tiny bottle of perfume for Ursula. He had never given a gift to any young girl and wondered if it was right to offer one to her. He would seek to meet her again when he returned to college and present her with the gift. His thoughts far away, he did not join in the conversation.

"Hey brother, lost somewhere? Dreaming of someone? Come on! Let us fix those bulbs before Mom and Dad return home from office! It should all be done by then, or Mom will create a big fuss. I had promised her we will do the job," called out Samir.

Good, obedient sons that they were, the two turned to the task at hand and had it all completed in time before the parents returned.

The bulbs were lit, lending a cheerful glow to the room as the family sat down for dinner that night. The spread consisted of both Indian and Western favorites. Over large helpings of butter chicken and naan brought by Nimisha from the Indian restaurant in town, accompanied by glasses of wine and finally followed by their Nani's contribution - 'pua', the Bihari sweet cooked by Sara under her direction - the talk became free and lively.

"It is time your elder one gets married. He has a good job, so what are you waiting for, Nimmi? Have you begun your search for a suitable girl yet?" asked Mrs.Misra.

"Well, it is not like India, Mamma. Sam will find someone himself. Why must I take the trouble?" laughed Nimisha.

"You hear that, Gopal? Trouble? What kind of mother is she? Not interested in finding a suitable bride for her son! Let me tell you, I know of enough families with beautiful daughters who would be delighted to find a smart, handsome groom like my Samir. A boy with a good job, too!

Why, they would come running to your house to offer you their daughters. With loads of money for dowry! Shall I spread the word around, about my most eligible grandson?"

Gopal smiled indulgently and shook his head. "Better ask Samir first if he is ready for marriage."

"How do you guys know if I don't already have a girl in mind?" teased Samir, "No 'deshi' Indian for me, Nani. And dowry? Don't even think of it, in this day and age, that too in America. I will marry a smart professional like my Mom."

"Thank you, beta," Nimisha acknowledged her son's compliment, "The choice is yours. A good housewife who can cook all the Indian food you like, or a smart working gal who will live on pizzas and sandwiches!"

"Well, I am happy with my professional wife," Gopal smiled warmly at Nimisha, "She has managed my home and family well, she is efficient both as a home maker and as a professional."

"Thanks, dear husband, you have been helpful too! I have no complaints," Nimisha replied.

"Oh well, let him choose his own bride, then," Mrs. Misra gave in, "Find your own girl, but choose an Indian, not a foreigner, that is all I ask."

It was here that Sandeep suddenly butted in. "But she can be part Indian, can't she, Nani?"

Later Sandeep wondered why he had asked that question. Was it because he had someone in mind? But no, he had never thought of Ursula that way. In fact she was just a casual acquaintance he enjoyed talking to, there was no question of there being anything more serious between them.

His question made his mother stare at him, a puzzled frown on her forehead while his father just shook his head. Samir gave him a wink and said teasingly, "Aha, already, that's fast work, dear brother!"

It was Nani who commented with a smile, "Half Indian can be anything. Depends on who the other half is! White American is welcome, for she will be really gora-chitta! But Sandeep, it is your brother's turn now, not yours, so be patient."

"Oh, I did not mean anything serious. I...I was just joking!" Embarrassed, Sandeep mumbled, but he continued to wonder. What had made him ask that question so suddenly and unexpectedly?

Chapter 15

The Gift

Sandeep remained conscious of the words he had let escape from his lips before his family at home. He remembered it when he met Ursula again at college. It made him feel awkward and shy. He found himself staring down at his hands to avoid meeting her eyes and felt his face going hot whenever she addressed him. Thank god, there were others around, and he did not have to talk face to face with her, he thought. Of course he had remembered to bring the gift, meant for her, with him. It was safely tucked inside his pocket, waiting for the right moment when he would present it to her.

The opportunity came soon enough, for their companions drifted away, one by one, to their rooms. Sandeep remained glued to his seat, quite deliberately, until the two were the only ones left on the table. Ursula must have understood his intentions, because she made no move to leave and sat firm, an expectant little smile playing around her shapely lips.

"Come on now, out with it. You wanted to say something?" she asked as soon as they were alone.

"Well, ahem, yes. I have a little something for you. A Christmas gift," he spoke softly and took out the gaily-wrapped box from his pocket.

"Oh, that is a great surprise. It is very nice of you. But....but...I must confess I do not have anything to give you...I am sorry. I didn't expect this...," she stammered.

"That's alright. Anyway, it is something very small. Hope you like it," murmured Sandeep.

"I am sure I will," she replied, her hands fiddling with the ribbon on the box. Soon she had untied it and removed the wrapping. "Perfume? Lovely!" She turned the box around, looked at the labels and exclaimed, "Perfect! Just the fragrance I love. Thank you so much!"

Before he could understand whether the remark was genuine or just plain courtesy, she had quickly jumped out of her seat and come closer to his. A sudden movement of her body, a swift bent and he felt the soft touch of lips against his cheek, as she gave him a light, fleeting kiss.

"Really sweet of you!" she whispered, "And good night now! Must return before my roommate starts wondering where I am!"

She left quickly, leaving him hot and embarrassed. Slowly, he walked towards his own room. "There you are! Why so late?" As usual, Ben Maddock was hunched on his bed, laptop on and music blaring as he played some game on his video.

"How does it matter to you? You stay up so late yourself! Let me also enjoy myself once in a while," retorted Sandeep.

"So where were you? With some girl?"

"Why should I tell you? Go on with your entertainment. It is bedtime for me!" said Sandeep. But it was not so easy to fall asleep. Though well protected with earplugs to keep away the disturbing noises emanating from the other bed, he kept awake, remembering with pleasure the light, soft brush of lips against his cheek and the fragrance of a presence so close to him he could have just clasped it to his chest. He blamed his tossing and turning to the video in the laptop, without understanding the actual reason.

He had lost his heart to the tall, lissome figure with the raven hair and green eyes. Her face kept flashing in and out through his half conscious mind until darkness closed in to banish it, and allowed him to fall asleep at last.

By the time Sandeep awoke, fresh and rejuvenated, his mind had latched on to the more mundane subjects that normally occupy a student's thoughts. He was late for his classes and saw that Ben had already left, leaving his bed and clothes in the usual mess. There was no time to tidy up his own part, and he was forced to follow his roommate's example. Quickly he brushed his teeth, grabbed a bar of energy food from his table and rushed to join his mates in class.

During classes he forced himself to pay attention and not to let his thoughts stray into distracting fields.

Fortunately the subjects he had to deal with that day were his favorites and the professors those he admired. He could focus well on their words and grasp it all without too much effort.

As the days passed Sandeep kept himself busy with his classes. He felt satisfied with himself for not allowing the girl to intrude into his thoughts.

It was Samir who reminded him about the girl again. As a good guardian and elder brother he had invited Sandeep to spend the weekend at his apartment in New York. The two had had a good time strolling down the shopping street, and ended the day at the Indian restaurant near his apartment.

"And now, what about the half Indian girl mentioned by you before Nani? Is there actually someone you know and like?" asked Samir as the two relaxed with the coffee after the meal.

"I know someone. But like? Sure I like many girls, as anyone would. But not in any special way! Of course not! What d'you think? That I am serious about someone? Not at all!" protested Sandeep most emphatically.

"I just asked. It is too early for you to think in those terms. You have to work hard at this stage in your life. You cannot afford to get distracted by girls," advised Samir in his elder brotherly voice.

"You don't have to tell me," laughed Sandeep, choosing not to take offence. After all, Samir was only doing his duty as his elder. He tried to change the subject. "Talking about studies, what would you advise about...?" he asked.

"Good question. This is what I think..." and Samir turned his attention towards more important matters, making the younger sibling sigh inwardly with relief.

The weekend passed without any further embarrassing queries. The two watched baseball on the greens, went to see a movie and had lunch at a pizza stall where Samir treated his brother to some good beer.

All in all, it was a real cool weekend. Sandeep was glad to have spent it in the company of his dear brother, for, busy with their own concerns, the two could get together only on rare occasions.

Chapter 16

"Speaking My Mind"

There was a sudden knock on the door and the two jumped towards it. Ben made it to the door first and quickly opened it. "Hi! What can I do for you?" Sandeep heard him ask politely as he stood behind him, curious to know who had come at this odd hour. They had just returned to their room after dinner at the common mess and were about to change and relax.

"I am looking for Sandeep Shukla. I was told this was his room. Is he in?" asked a female voice and Sandeep pushed Ben aside to rush to the door.

"Yes, yes. This is our room, Ursula. What brings you here?" he asked.

She stood there with another girl and he could feel his heart give a lurch as he met her eyes. He was seeing her after a long time, busy as he had been with various activities.

"Hi, Sandeep! I have come to invite you... actually there is to be a "Speaking my Mind" occasion that I am organizing at college on Saturday next week. We have invited some...ahem... eminent seniors to talk to us on various topics. I thought of you as I had heard you that day. You had spoken so well. Will you join us for the function? Here is the program!" She thrust a printed card at him and said, "Hope the date suits you. Do try to come."

Sandeep glanced at the details. There were several subjects on the agenda and he looked up questioningly. "So which one am I assigned to?"

"Take your pick. You are the first one we are approaching. I am giving you the first choice, you see," she said.

"Umm, ask my friend also. This is Ben Maddock, my roommate. He has great ideas too, and expresses them quite strongly. Highly recommended by yours truly!"

Ursula turned her attention to Ben who had been standing quietly in the background so far. He came forward now and smiled at the girls, "Ben Maddock, at your service," he gave an exaggerated bow, "Will be happy to put forward my thoughts. That is, if you consider them to be worthwhile."

Ursula smiled and introduced herself and her friend. "Pleased to meet you. I am Ursula Pershad and this is my friend, Angela Brown. We request you to join us for a special talk session that I have organized. It will consist of discussions on subjects of special concern to us first year students. We invite experienced senior guys to tell us what they feel about these important subjects. The aim is to initiate a dialogue between juniors and seniors. Get the idea?"

"Sure I do!" Ben had his eyes fixed on Angela, who smiled back, revealing dazzling white teeth against shiny, smooth, ebony skin.

"We want guys to be sympathetic towards female concerns. Women empowerment is what I was thinking of for you, Sandeep. You spoke so well about it that day. I would like you to talk on the subject again. Would you, please?"

"Yes, why not? I do believe in gender equality and will be happy to speak again, if that is what you want. At least, I will not have to prepare for it, for I am familiar with the subject."

"Great! What about you, Ben?"

"Uhh, let me think. Discrimination? I have faced it sometimes, and hate it when distinction is made on the basis of the color of one's skin. Black is beautiful, that is what I say! And I assert this strongly. What say you, Angela, agree?"

"Sure. Am proud of my skin color," Angela stretched out her bare, shapely arms to let the boys admire them, which they duly did, though silently.

"Done then. I am putting down both your names. Don't forget, the coming Saturday, at 4 p.m. And don't change your minds and let us down, I will never forgive you, if you do so," warned Ursula, with a laugh.

"How can we forget? We look forward to it, in fact," Sandeep assured them, as the girls bid them goodnight.

The boys were excited about the event and discussed it between themselves before the day arrived. Ben related some painful experiences that he had faced as a teenager at school. "When they wanted to hurt me for some reason or the other they hurled the word 'Blackie' at me. I was stronger and more powerful than many of them, who probably felt it was the only way they could get back at me. It would make me really mad!" remembered Ben.

"It did not happen to me, for some reason," said Sandeep thoughtfully, "But I remember it took some time for my classmates to be friendly with me. There....there was a kind of a wall....between them and me, until they realized I was just another boy like any of them. And then they became close and friendly."

Saturday arrived soon enough and the two roommates eagerly entered the Hall where the function was being held. It was a full hall, occupied by excited first year boys and girls, who clapped enthusiastically as the seniors were presented before them, one by one.

There were talks on various subjects, ranging from politics to career options to the need for pursuing excellence, and the importance of hard work for achieving it. First year students asked questions and were answered gravely by the seniors. When it was Sandeep's turn he stood up confidently to speak.

"First of all, thanks for inviting me here," began Sandeep. He caught Ursula's eye and smiled before he went on, "Women are precious beings. We men admire as well as adore them for the role they play in our lives. Where would we men be if not for them – mothers, wives, lovers!" he paused as a restless wave swept the rows of seats where the female audience sat, scowling at him. He glanced at the raised eyebrows on Ursula's face and laughed, "Ha, ha! I knew my words would annoy some of you, but I was about to add other stuff too. Well, not just the above roles but also as – our partners, often our superiors at work and bosses too at office! So why do I consider them to be admirable? Because they are really superwomen! Not only are they good at what they do for their families, children and homes; they are just as capable in fields other than this, at businesses, in the corporate world and in offices where they carry on just as efficiently. Both as wives, mothers, home makers, and at offices, as soldiers, scientists, even as space walkers, they can do everything that a male can boast of doing. So why not consider them to be not just equal; but way superior to us lower beings! No, I am not joking or making fun of you ladies. That is not at all my intention. Please, I say this seriously," he paused and smiled.

"You must believe me, because my words are based on experience – yes, it is my mother that I now speak of. She is a successful professional. But she has looked after us – my brother and me, and of course my father – so well! With love, concern and care! We never felt her absence! That is what being a woman means!" he added and waited for the clapping to end.

Encouraged by the response, Sandeep went on to mention several other women who had struggled and achieved success in various fields, whether politics, art, medicine or science, until he had won the hearts of all the girls in the hall. He concluded by calling for a big hand for the females in the audience, who, he said, stood for the new generation of women. "Ladies who are destined to soon rule the world and make it a better place for all citizens," he said, ending his long speech.

His words made the listeners, half of whom were girls, jump up enthusiastically to give him a standing ovation.

Ben Maddock followed after him. "Let me put it clearly in black and white," he said with a chuckle, "America, no doubt, is a nation of blacks and whites. At one time there was a world of difference between people of the two colours but, thanks to those who struggled to bring equality, we can now say that we may be very different in appearance but we do have equality of opportunity for every citizen of our great nation." He paused, while a burst of claps greeted his words. "That is how I am here, in this college where only a lucky few may get admission. Born a black, I now stand shoulder to shoulder with my white brethren. I can go on to become an honored professor at college. As long as I am prepared to work diligently I can reach great heights, just as any other student here can. That is the beauty of this country. Of course, there are some who do not agree and trouble us. We must ignore them. So I tell you, blacks, or people of any color – browns, yellows and reds - raise high your heads and do not consider yourself to be inferior to anyone. You can do it. You will do it. Have the confidence, no matter what some might say, and I well know, several may not agree – but you are just as good as anyone else here!"

The crowd rose and clapped wildly for him.

It was a satisfying day for both the senior students. After the thanks and other formalities were over, Ursula and

Angela met the two outside the Hall. "That was good. Hope you enjoyed the interaction as much as we did?" asked Ursula.

The two assured them that they had.

"We loved your talk!" said the two girls enthusiastically.

"I have had some bad experiences at school. They used to disturb me a great deal and made me feel so inferior. I am glad you gave a boost to my self esteem, made me feel I was just the same as anyone else, whether black, brown, white or yellow!" gushed Angela, smiling at Ben, who looked pleased.

"We are all equal in this great, big world. There should not be any distinctions of class, caste, gender or color. As long as one is prepared to work hard, all can aspire to reach the sky. Isn't it?" asked Ursula enthusiastically.

"Yes. That is how it should be. We are all human beings, created by the same superior being," added Angela. The others nodded in agreement.

For Sandeep, it was a most satisfying occasion. He hoped many others would follow.

Chapter 17

Wedding Arrangements

College days passed quickly in a flurry of activity, with sports, studies and other activities occupying the students' time and attention. Soon another year was over. The seniors had graduated while the juniors had moved up another rung towards graduation.

Sandeep's parents came over to participate in his graduation ceremony. His brother, Samir, too, joined the family, along with a girl they had not met before. "Meet Pamela!" he informed them with a smile, "She is a colleague, who works in my office."

Sandeep looked at the stranger with interest mixed with curiosity. Though dressed in Western wear the girl looked very much an Indian, with her pale brown skin, brown eyes and short, black hair. She greeted the elders with a polite 'namaste'.

The next sentence from Samir astonished them all. "And let me inform you, everybody - Pamela has accepted my proposal to be a partner for life!" he said in an excited rush of words.

"Oh, this is a surprise, indeed!" cried Nimisha, her voice a mixture of shock, delight and excitement. She stared at the newcomer, who blushed and lowered her eyes modestly.

"You never told us about her!" complained Gopal, but added warmly the next moment, "However, welcome. We must get to know each other. Good you brought her here to meet your family."

"And this is my brother, Sandeep. You may call him Sandy," Samir turned to introduce his sibling, patting him affectionately on the shoulder.

"Hi!" responded the boy.

The girl smiled at Sandeep. "Hi, I am Pamela Roy." She had lost her shyness by now and addressed her elders more confidently, "Happy to meet you all! Sam has spoken to me often about each of you. I know you well already!" she told them. The elders, curious to learn more about the new entrant to the family, badgered the girl with questions that she answered with great patience.

"What do your parents do?" Nimisha asked the usual question.

"My father is a doctor in a hospital in New York while my mother is a home maker. She looked after us four kids very diligently and made us all do well at school. I am grateful to her for staying at home to look after us," Pamela gave full credit to her mother, knowing well that Samir's mother was, unlike hers, a professional whose first preference was her career.

"Well, our mother is a career woman. But it certainly does not mean we became failures at academics!" protested Sandeep, ready to take up cudgels on his parents' behalf.

Gopal, realising that matters could result in some hard feelings in a relationship just about to begin, hastened to quench the argument. "Every person has the right to take a decision on this, I guess. Preferring to be a home -maker is also a woman's prerogative; she has every right to decide about that, Sandeep. Allow a woman that freedom, without being prejudiced against it!" he said with a laugh.

His tactful interference succeeded in turning the conversation to safer subjects, which included talk about Sandeep's plans for his future. What did he plan to do, now that he had graduated? Study further, or try finding an internship somewhere? Would he stay on at New York or return home to Chicago and do something there?

"Your Nani is looking forward to your return. She could not come, as she was not feeling too well. But she misses you both and says it would be great if at least one child returned home to stay with us," explained Nimisha.

"So what are your future plans, Sandeep?" asked Gopal.

His father's words brought his attention back to Ursula. Sandeep realized he did not want to go too far from her, work or no work, job or no job. He felt he just could not bear separation from her. However, his father's question reminded him - it was time he decided what he really wanted to do with his life. It had to be something that allowed him to stay on in close proximity to the person he was slowly but surely falling head over heels in love with.

So what would be ideal for him? He well knew that his parents, quintessential Indian immigrants that they were, certainly expected him to follow family tradition and find a decent, well paying job for himself.

The thoughts raced through Sandeep's mind as he sat mute before the questioning faces. Not receiving a reply from the pensive boy, Gopal turned to his other son. "And what about you? Sandy seems uncertain still. You are already settled as far as a job is concerned. So now it is time to take the next step. I mean, marriage! Any plans for it?"

"Well, I am ready for it. Any time you all decide!" Samir gave a broad smile and replied with alacrity, happy at being asked the crucial question.

"We would like to meet Pamela's parents before anything is decided," said Nimisha, "If they are in New York, maybe we can meet while we are here."

"Good idea! Ask them to do so, Sam," ordered Gopal.

"Sure!" was the quick reply.

The Roys turned up the very next day to meet the Shuklas in their hotel room. Tall and jovial Diwakar Roy was a medical practitioner, while his diminutive, demure wife, clad in an orange South silk sari with a gold border, was a housewife, as Pamela had informed them earlier. Following them quietly was Pamela, dressed in a pink and blue salwar suit with a blue chunni draped modestly around her shoulders. The two men shook hands warmly.

''It is our privilege to meet you, Sir," said Diwakar Roy, extending the courtesy he well knew was expected to be given to the future father-in-law of his daughter, according to good old Indian custom.

"Our pleasure," returned Gopal politely.

Nimisha, a glaring contrast in her navy blue jacket and trousers to the sari clad lady, led the other woman away from the men, and, to make her feel more at ease, invited her to sit beside her on the sofa opposite. Samir and Sandeep sat together next to Pamela in the corner, respectfully watching their parents converse gravely with each other.

After exchanging further polite enquiries about each other's family backgrounds, including their places of origin, details of ancestors and members resident in the US along with their professions and so on, the talk at last turned to the subject they had come to discuss.

"You have a smart and very eligible son," began Diwakar, "Our daughter is also very talented. We are indeed fortunate that the two have agreed to marry each other."

"We too, are very happy that they have made up their minds to marry. You indeed have a lovely and talented daughter," responded Gopal, not to be outdone, "We are glad to welcome her as our dear daughter-in-law, and I am sure my wife is delighted, too."

"It will be great to have the main ceremony here in New York," broke in Mrs. Roy, eager to have her say, "Hope that is fine with you."

"Oh no!" protested Nimisha quickly, "My mother is too old and frail to travel. She would love to attend her elder grandson's wedding, the first in the family. She is so excited about it, will not like to miss it for anything. It would be more convenient if we could have a grand function at our place in Chicago. We have a fairly large house in the suburbs, with a huge compound, so it won't be a problem at all," she rushed through the speech, before the other woman could put in a word.

"Oh, but..." began Mrs. Roy and looked helplessly at her husband, who quickly came to her rescue, "It is not such a great problem, dear, we can have two functions, one here and another at Chicago."

"No, no!" insisted Nimisha,"You do not know my mother. She would not like to miss either, and will insist on attending both functions, which will lead to all kinds of problems both for us and for her. And then who has the time? We are both busy in our respective jobs. One combined reception will have to do, and in Chicago rather than in New York."

As is usual, the bride's side had to bow before the wishes of the boy's parents. It was decided finally to have a joint reception, to be held at Chicago. The fixing of the date also led to much argument, as Mrs. Roy believed in consulting astrologers to find the right time for the auspicious occasion, while Nimisha and Gopal were quite dismissive of the idea. The time must be decided according to their work schedules rather than on the remote stars that shone from a distant sky.

After much discussion and polite debate, the right date was at last finalized, much to the relief of the younger listeners, by now thoroughly bored with the elders' arguments.

Chapter 18

The Wedding

At last it was time to say goodbye to Ursula. Sandeep met the girl over coffee at their favourite restaurant. "So, are you returning home for the vacations, or planning to go somewhere?" she asked him.

"Well, I will go home first. Relax for a while and ponder over the question - what next?" Sandeep replied with a laugh.

"You mean you have not thought about it yet?" Ursula looked shocked. "Why, many others I have talked to have it all chalked out. They know just where they are going."

"Well, I am not like everyone else! Why should I be?" Sandeep asked, "I am very much my own person. But tell me, what are you doing during the vacation?"

"Traveling. Visiting friends. There is one at Chicago also. I might visit her, too. If you are there, we can see each other," said Ursula, to Sandeep's great joy.

"Oh, that's wonderful! Do come. My brother is to wed there next month, as I have told you. It will be just awesome if you joined us!" Sandeep was truly delighted at the prospect.

"Would love to attend - haven't been to an Indian wedding....well, did attend one, but long ago, when I was a child. Would be fun, I am sure," Ursula said enthusiastically.

Sandeep gave her the date, venue and the time for the wedding. "You must come," he insisted.

"I will make my travel plan accordingly. I will definitely be there," promised Ursula.

The wedding was to be held a month later on an auspicious day, as insisted upon by the bride's side. The venue, as decided by Nimisha, was the Shukla home in Chicago. Her house was large and the grounds spacious enough to accommodate all the guests, she had informed the others. Though normally it was the bride's home that hosted a wedding, the Roys were happy to take up the offer. It would save them the effort of finding a place large enough to accommodate invitees from both sides for the joint wedding.

It was the Roys who had found an experienced Indian priest to conduct the ceremony. "He knows the "shlokas" and is able to chant them well in the right intonation. In fact this 'pandit' has conducted wedding ceremonies for many of our relatives' and friends' children," Mrs. Roy had explained.

Preparations for the wedding kept the Shuklas occupied until the day fixed for the ceremony. Invitations were sent out to relatives living far away in India as well as to those residing in the USA, arrangements made to host those who would arrive from distant places, menus fixed and preparations made for hosting festive meals for the invitees, decorations and music selected and ordered – and several other tasks had to be completed before the final wedding day arrived.

At last all was ready. A bright, golden day dawned in mid July, when the trees looked fresh and green, and rainbow hued blooms nodded and smiled at the sun shining bright in the blue sky. The guests, resplendent in rich gowns and colorful saris, glittering in their diamond and gold jewelry, began to arrive in the afternoon. The men wore long sherwanis and silk scarves around their necks; others were in formal suits and ties. Samir, as the groom, was clad in a rich brocade sherwani in maroon and gold, while Sandeep, as the groom's brother, was no less richly dressed in his silver and navy blue sherwani.

The Shukla mansion, as well as its sprawling compound, was tastefully decorated for the wedding. Garlands of fragrant flowers were strung between pillars wrapped in red silk, while every tree had strings of glistening bulbs waiting to be lighted as soon as the sun dipped low in the horizon. The whole place had indeed turned into a magical fairytale palace.

To add to the air of festivity there was a band playing loud music, interspersed by recorded melodies. Lilting wedding songs from Indian films, fast Punjabi pop as well as naughty Bhojpuri lyrics, and popular Western music provided a medley of delightful sounds in the background.

The elders, including Sandeep's grandmother in her heavy, mustard colored, Benarasi silk sari, welcomed the Roys when they arrived in a big group, resplendent in as much finery as the Shuklas. The bride wore a long, flaring, pink 'lehnga' embellished with gold embroidery, while a pink, chiffon 'chunari', sprinkled with golden stars veiled her beautiful face. She walked with delicate, graceful steps towards the 'mandap' or canopy of flowers under which the wedding ceremonies were to be held. The 'pandit' welcomed her and invited Samir also to sit under the canopy.

The ceremonies soon began. Sandeep, who knew that the process would last for some time, hastened back to the entrance, where he waited anxiously for Ursula to enter. She had promised she would attend, but had not arrived as yet. He paced up and down, wondering, hoping she would keep her promise and turn up.

There she was, at last! Sandeep hurried to the gate to welcome her. His heart thumped in excitement, for he was seeing her after several weeks. As he approached the two girls, he noted once again with a wild jump to his heart, how ravishing she looked. Both the girls were dressed for the occasion in Indian dresses, but the boy had eyes only for Ursula. Her green, flowing 'lehnga' and 'chunari' made her green eyes sparkle brighter while the long emeralds dangling from her ears were tantalizingly inviting. Diamonds and emeralds lined her white, slender throat.

"Finally!" exclaimed Sandeep, "What took you so long?"

"It is a pretty long drive from the city center. Your home is so far, we did not know it would take us so long to reach," explained Ursula.

"Ok, never mind. The ceremonies have begun. Come and watch ... they must be wondering where I am," said Sandeep, as he led them towards the 'mandap' where all his relatives had gathered. Pamela's father was now seated next to the bride and groom, for he had a role to play, too. The women sang merry wedding songs to the beat of a 'dholak', the Indian drum. Sandeep found some empty seats for his guests and sat down next to Ursula.

"So you have found friends here too?" spoke a voice. It was his grandmother, Mrs. Mishra, who gazed with interest at the two girls seated beside him. Sandeep hastened to introduce them to the old lady.

"My friend, Ursula, and this is her friend, Melissa, whom Ursula has come to visit, all the way from New York. And ladies, this is my grandmother," he explained to the visitors.

"Lovely girls!" exclaimed Mrs. Mishra, glancing pointedly at Ursula, "Are you Indian? Is she the girl you mentioned the other day at our Christmas dinner?"

Sandeep did not know where to look. "Uh...huh, Nani. What.... when?" he pretended, turning red and stammering embarrassedly.

"My father is Indian, my mother is not!" Ursula gave a short, practised reply.

Sandeep knew she did not like such intrusions into her privacy and quickly tried to divert everyone's attention. "Look, they are walking around the fire. Let's listen to the Pandit. He is telling them to repeat the vows they must make to each other before they become a couple."

"Oh, that's interesting!" exclaimed Melissa, who was attending an Indian wedding for the very first time. She watched, fascinated, as the groom and the bride walked solemnly around the fire burning in the centre of the 'mandap', or canopy. The delightful aroma of ghee sprinkled over the fire filled their nostrils, while the sound of the women singing wedding songs resounded in their ears. After each round, the couple stopped to repeat the words pronounced by the priest.

"The wedding vows," commented Sandeep, "I believe there are seven of them."

"But what are those vows? That they make to each other?" asked Melissa, curious.

"Oh, to care for each other, I suppose," laughed Sandeep, dismissing her query, for he had no idea, never having bothered about the details of an Indian wedding.

"But you should know, dear boy," Mrs. Mishra, who had overheard the conversation, butted in to scold him.

"Alright, you explain then, Nani," replied Sandeep.

"Well, first the groom vows to take care of and provide for the wife. She promises to look after their home. The second is that the groom promises to protect their home and kids. In return, the girl promises to be happy when he is happy. The third is about praying together for prosperity and spiritual fulfillment. The fourth is to together seek blessings for the whole family. And...," Nani was explaining when Sandeep cut her short.

"In brief, it is all about being loyal to each other, and for caring together for the well being of both themselves and the family, you see," he interrupted. "Finally, they declare themselves to be husband and wife, and pledge to be companions for life."

"So sweet and romantic," murmured Melissa, while Pamela nodded enthusiastically. Sandeep, however, had, by this time, lost interest. "Ok, ok, Nani, we understand ..." he repeated impatiently, "It is all about being a good, loyal couple, faithful to each other. Now look, another important ceremony!"

Their attention diverted, the girls watched in silence as the groom went on to fill the bride's parting with red powder. The two were now well and truly married. The women gathered there burst into a congratulatory Bhojpuri song, accompanied as before by the rhythmic beat of the 'dholak', to bless the newly wedded couple.

The rituals were over at last.

The guests all made a beeline for the lavishly laid out buffet. The band struck up once again and couples began to enjoy the party, dancing, chatting and having a great time. Sandeep introduced his two guests to the others, including to his parents, who accepted the girls' presence without any questions, unlike his inquisitive grandmother. He tried to steer them away from her whenever she happened to be close to them.

It was not so easy, for the old lady sought them out whenever she could. "Is she your girl friend?" was the next query she made.

"Umm. They are both my friends," replied Sandeep.

"The one who has come all the way from New York must be a very special friend," the old lady was annoyingly persistent.

"We are in the same college campus. She was visiting her friend in Chicago, so she came to see me too," explained the grandson.

"You must have invited her, of course," insisted his grandmother.

"Yes. She wanted to see an Indian wedding, so I asked her to come."

"But you are half Indian, so you must have attended many. Haven't you?" she turned to Ursula again.

"Not really, we don't have many relatives....," replied the girl.

"How is that? All of us have so many relatives spread all across Amrika. All in well paying jobs too. What about your parents? What do they do?" was the next part of the inquisition.

"Umm....my father is in the hospitality business....," mumbled Ursula reluctantly, as observed by Sandeep. It was the first time he had heard this. He had never thought of asking her about her background. There was so much else to talk about and, in any case, he had hardly cared about what her parents did. It was of no consequence to him, as long as they themselves got along well with each other, which they certainly did. Once again he tried to change the subject. "Have you heard that song? It is an old one, sung by Michael Jackson. I used to love it!"

And the subject turned towards popular songs they had both known. Mrs. Mishra, interested no longer, turned towards another lady who had just greeted her. She smiled back and the two older ladies began to chat.

Sandeep seized the opportunity to steer the two girls away from his inquisitive grandmother and towards more congenial company.

It was fun time after this, for the music and the dancing continued as the moon came up and the stars twinkled in the midnight blue screen overhead. The heavenly bodies, however, looked pale before the glitter and glimmer of the celebrations below.

And for the bedazzled young man it turned out to be a night that he would never forget.

Chapter 19

Sandeep's Decision

Melissa had been whisked away in the arms of a friend she had happened to meet at the party. Ursula and Sandeep were left alone together to enjoy every dance that the band struck up. As time passed, the lights were dimmed; the band began to play older, more romantic songs with slower beats. Couples drew closer together. Each number brought Sandeep and Ursula nearer to each other - closer and closer - till the two moved together cheek to cheek and heart to heart. The fragrance of the perfume she wore, which he recognized as the one he had gifted her for Christmas, filled all his senses. Her breath caressed his cheeks softly. The combination that her physical closeness, the steady beat of the music, and the soft lights above, brought him into a heady state of carelessness. Nothing mattered except her closeness. He clasped her tighter still in his arms and bending down, kissed her full on the lips, something he had not dared to do as yet.

She did not resist him. Instead she bent her head backwards, clung tighter and returned his kiss with as much passion as he had done. It was a moment that lasted perhaps for a few seconds, but brought them bliss such as they had never experienced before. Slowly, reluctantly, they drew apart. There was nothing to be said, for those few seconds of passion had said it all. Their love stood fully revealed, admitted and acknowledged.

Soon they were deep in an enchanted world of their own, their bodies moving together in perfect harmony with each other. At last, tired, but with his heart leaping wildly, Sandeep led a dazed Ursula to a secluded corner bench where they sat together, silent because no words were needed; everything had been said. Here they sat, shoulders touching, hands in each other's, while they tried to calm their beating hearts.

"Hey, where did you two vanish?" a sudden shout broke the magic. It was Melissa. "We have been looking for you. People are leaving; it is quite late. Don't you think we should go too?"

Sandeep jumped up, followed by Ursula. "Oh! I did not know it was so late. Yes, time to leave," she cried.

The magic moment gone, they were back into the normal world.

"Where are your parents? We must thank them and bid them goodbye," said Melissa. The three found their hosts standing near the gate, seeing off their guests. The Shukla's, who saw the two girls as their son's special friends, sent them off with warm hugs

Sandeep returned to the house, the excitement and the joy of the evening still warming his heart. He found his grandmother, exhausted after the party, reclining on the sofa. She perked up as soon as he entered, sat up straight, and welcomed him with a bright smile. "So it was not at all a chance remark? You do have a girl friend! Very pretty, I am impressed - she is so fair, looks so American and yet has Indian blood. Good choice, dear boy. Indeed, you have chosen well!"

"Come on Nani, things do not move so fast. She is just a friend. Nothing more," protested Sandeep, his cheeks red, as if caught in some criminal act.

"Ha, ha! It is okay. You do not have to hide it. And you have my full approval, so go ahead and marry her, my dear!"

"No, no, Nani. Marriage? Who is talking of marriage? She is just a friend from college," protested Sandeep. He quickly walked away before she could make any further remarks.

As he lay in bed and remembered his grandmother's words, the very idea of marriage seemed too farfetched to consider. With a little laugh he dismissed the idea altogether. After all, he had to study further and settle down into some profession before thinking of something as binding as a betrothal. Well did he know that Ursula would dismiss the whole idea without giving it another thought; she still had a year to go before her graduation.

Of one thing, however, Sandeep was sure. He had to stay somewhere in New York, so that he could meet Ursula whenever he needed to. This thought helped him make up his mind for he now had an aim. He had been offered, while on campus, an internship in an advertising firm in an international company based in New York. He decided now to accept that offer. The new assignment would give him ample scope for being creative and making good use of his ability to communicate ideas convincingly to others. And, most important, he could remain near Ursula.

When he informed his parents about his plan to intern in New York, Nimisha expressed satisfaction that her son had finally made up his mind about his future. Gopal considered the idea thoughtfully. "Not bad. I guess it can work out to be a good alternative to the usual jobs we Indians take up. No harm in having a go at it. You must be happy doing whatever you decide on. I am sure you will do well if it is something you like working on. Hard work and passion will lead you to success in whatever you undertake. So go ahead and follow your heart, son. Our best wishes to you," he finally said, patting his son's shoulders encouragingly.

Sandeep nodded happily. Approval from his parents was of great importance to him. He had been worrying about their reactions and felt relieved to get the go ahead from them.

"But I was looking forward to my grandson staying on at home and finding something to do here, so that he could be with us," his grandmother looked dismayed, "Why must he return to New York?"

"He cannot be tied to his mother's and grandmother's apron strings all his life!" laughed Gopal, "But don't you feel bad. I am sure he will come often and meet you, Mamma dear."

Chapter 20

An Indian Dinner

Sandeep joined the company as soon as his vacations were over. He made it a point to find a room close to the campus where Ursula stayed. The two continued to meet, more often than they had done earlier. It was a pleasant year for both. Whenever she found time she would come over and stay with Sandeep in his digs. Soon all their friends knew that the two often spent their nights together; so did his brother Samir, who now lived with his wife in an apartment in the city. Pamela, who continued to work in the office with Samir, often invited her brother-in-law home to have dinner with them. Sandeep, on his part, took Ursula along whenever he visited his brother. He was glad to see that she and Pamela got along well together.

It was Pamela who showed the most curiosity about Ursula's family. The brothers, along with the two girls, were out for dinner together during a weekend when all four happened to be free, a rare occasion indeed. They were in an Indian restaurant, where they ordered the typical chicken tikka masala, along with tandoori roti, that most Americans are familiar with.

"Do you like Indian food?" asked Pamela as she bit into the succulent, spicy leg of the chicken.

"Not always. Sometimes it is too spicy for me," smiled Ursula.

"Arre, what kind of an Indian are you, that you do not appreciate spicy stuff?" Pamela looked surprised, "It makes me wonder. Which parent is Indian and where is the other parent from?"

Sandeep did not like these blunt questions to be asked but Ursula replied with an amused smile. "My father is from India and my mother is from Poland. Her parents came over years ago, before my mother was born, and so she was brought up here as an American citizen," she explained.

"Oh! Then you may be more used to European food, which is quite mild compared to our stuff! No wonder you find this food too spicy!" exclaimed Pamela.

"I do eat Indian, too, as my father runs restaurants that specialize in Indian cuisine, specially from the eastern part of the country. But my mother cooks her own favourites at home and I find that I like her cooking more," Ursula replied.

"Hey, Samir, we must taste food at her Dad's place sometime!" cried Pamela enthusiastically, "Is there one in New York?"

"Yes. In Queens, where there are many more Indians. But we have other food joints in New Jersey where my family lives. You know that area is full of Indians who have settled there," explained Ursula.

"Let's meet at your New York restaurant some time then. It will be fun!" declared Pamela. The others had no objection.

And so it was that the next get-together of the foursome took place at the Indian restaurant belonging to Ursula's father. The staff immediately recognized Ursula, who had been there before with her father, and rushed to them to give her and her guests due attention and a very special treatment.

The chef himself came to their table to take down their orders while waiters hovered around their table to serve them.

"What would you like, Ma'am? As you know, we have a diverse menu – from all four corners of India," asked the chef.

"North, South, East or West, guys?" Ursula turned to her guests to inquire.

"We have enough of tandooris and chicken tikka masalas," began Samir, "Let's have something different."

"Idli, dosa and sambhar, too, are common," added Pamela.

"How about pav-bhaji or poha from the West then?" questioned the chef.

"What else is there? Something different?" asked Sandeep.

"If all agree, do try the Bihari litti-chokha. It is an unusual dish, and a speciality of our restaurants. I shall also recommend a good lamb dish to go with it, a hot lamb curry," the chef told them.

"Alright, if you recommend it. Surely you would know," said Samir.

The menu decided, the four settled down to enjoy the dinner. Ursula suggested other items that would go with the main one and the meal turned out to be quite a feast.

As he did every time they went out, Sandeep escorted Ursula back to her room in the college. This gave the two enough 'alone time' to chat and enjoy each other's company. They held hands as they boarded the train back home, and as they walked down the dark, shady lane that led to her room Sandeep drew Ursula closer to him. Between kisses and embraces it took the two quite a while to arrive at their destination. More time was spent lingering at the entrance to bid each other goodbye before Sandeep left, reluctantly, to return to his own place.

A few days later, when he met Ursula again Sandeep found her looking pale and distressed.

"Anything the matter?" he asked solicitously, touching her cheeks with tender fingers.

"Don't you think we should tell our parents about us? Or, is our relationship just something casual for you?" she asked.

Sandeep was startled out of his comfort zone. For him the two were good friends and he did intend it to last forever, but he had not considered it to be of importance to anyone else except them. "Does it matter?" he asked.

"You know it does to traditional parents. Maybe not to you or me, but most Indians cannot think of any relationship between a girl and a boy except in terms of their marriage," explained Ursula.

"Who cares?" Sandeep shrugged off her statement.

"I do," said Ursula softly.

"What does that mean?" asked Sandeep, surprised at her admission that it mattered to her.

Ursula turned to face him squarely. "Let me explain. Actually someone has informed my father that we are... Err... umm...spending our nights together. He seemed to be quite shocked at the idea. Rang me up, asked me who it was, and what was the boy's intention, warned me not to get entangled with such boys and... to cut it short, made quite a fuss. Don't be angry. Actually I know he is quite a traditionalist, but..."

"OK. Get the idea. He is an old fashioned dude. Doesn't know that it is nothing to make him feel so shocked about. Happens all the time," complained Sandeep.

"Well, it may be quite normal for us young people. But the elders are not used to such freedom and disapprove of it. So ... what do we do about it, Sandeep?" questioned Ursula, a worried frown on her face.

"What do you want me to do?" countered Sandeep.

"Meet him! Let him see you are no criminal, but just a decent young man with no evil intentions," suggested Ursula promptly.

"No problem. Always ready to fulfill my sweetheart's wishes!" said Sandeep, with an exaggerated bow and a laugh, "I am willing to present myself before your esteemed father. Ok? Happy?" He pinched her cheek lightly.

The expression of relief and joy on her face made Sandeep realize how worried she had been. He put his arm around her shoulder and gave her a warm hug. She responded by looking up at him with eyes that had become large and misty. "I hate to see you look unhappy," whispered Sandeep tenderly, bending down to plant a gentle kiss on her brow.

"Thanks, dearest. Love you," murmured Ursula.

A few moments later the two separated from each other's arms at last, their moods back to normal. Smiling in relief, Sandeep held her hand and led her towards his room. "And now for our night of orgy before your father decides to put an end to it, in case he does not approve of me," he teasingly laughed.

The incident made Sandeep realize that he could not continue to take his relationship with Ursula lightly. He certainly wanted to spend the rest of his life with her, but perhaps it was time to put a name to it, to acknowledge that she was his girl forever and ever. Marriage was still out of the question no doubt, but in the meantime he had to let everyone know she was his girl and he was committed fully to her. He must stake his claim on her before her family thought of betrothing her to someone else. If her father was conservative enough to worry about whom she was going out with, it would not be surprising if he tried to impose his choice of a suitable groom on her. He had heard that in India girls were forced to marry according to their parents' wishes. No, no, before that happened, he must meet the family and impress on them that he was just the right boy for their precious daughter.

He realized that the old man, Ursula's father, had to meet and accept him before he allowed his daughter to do so. Not only this, if they spent their nights in each other's arms, as he had been informed, the old guy needed to feel confident that they would wed each other later, when the time came.

As far as Sandeep himself was concerned, there was no doubt in his mind. By now he was absolutely sure - he wanted Ursula to be his companion for life 'till death doth pull them apart'. Which, of course, meant marriage! And he well knew what that involved, after the vows he had heard the bride and groom take together around the holy fire.

It was a sacred commitment that a man and a woman made, not only towards each other, but also towards the generations that came after them. To love and to care, to remain loyal and faithful to each other, to protect and look after a family - being together just now meant all this in the future.

Yes, it was serious and a big responsibility that he was taking on at this stage in his life. He fell silent and thought about its consequences. No, it was not a burden. On the other hand, a thrill of excitement ran through his body at the thought. He knew he wanted it with all his heart, body and soul.

Yes, it was Ursula whom he wanted to marry, to be his companion for life.

Chapter 21

A Great Shock

"Have you definitely made up your mind about the girl?" asked Samir, whom the younger brother finally decided to consult.

"Yes. She is the person I want to spend my life with," Sandeep nodded emphatically and with great certainty.

"Go ahead and marry her then. I will help..." offered Samir.

"No, no. I do intend to marry her, but it is too early for it. We will marry later, when we are both better settled," protested his brother.

"So what do you want to do then?"

"Be together. Without anyone objecting... I mean, her parents. Ursula told me that her father is shocked to hear about us. He does not like the idea of our spending nights together, as we... we sometimes do," admitted Sandeep, blushing a deep red.

"Oho, I see!" winked Samir with a little smile. "A serious problem indeed! Tell you what? Her father may be old-fashioned, but I know our parents are modern enough not to mind. Did you know that Mom and Dad are coming over this weekend to be with Pamela, who is unwell?"

"Is she ill? What happened?" Sandeep expressed his concern.

"Nothing serious. Just the usual, when you are expecting," replied Samir.

"Oh!" It took a few moments for Sandeep to understand. "I see. Great. Congratulations!"

"So I will persuade Mom and Dad to visit your friend's parents. I am sure they would feel reassured... at least enough to allow their daughter to... well, carry on with you. Until you are ready to get married, that is," suggested Samir.

"Sounds fine, provided Mom and Dad agree. Do you think they will?" wondered Sandeep doubtfully.

"Sure they will. And why should they not? They have already met Ursula. Everyone seemed to like her, including Nani, the most difficult one to please. I remember her saying that you had made a good choice. And if she feels that way, I think Mom would, too," Samir reassured his troubled younger brother, and was happy to see the worried cloud lift from his face.

Sandeep felt grateful to his brother for understanding and sympathizing with him. It certainly made him feel a little better. He began to look forward eagerly to his parents' visit.

Samir was as good as his word. He persuaded his parents to meet Ursula's family. Not only this, he spoke to Ursula and requested her to fix up a meeting between the two sets of parents. He had it all planned out before the

Shuklas arrived in New York the next Saturday. After they had rested a day or two, they were ready to undertake the trip to Ursula's home in New Jersey.

"It's really crazy," grumbled Nimisha, as the family settled down in the car being driven by Samir. Soon they were speeding up the highway leading out of the city. "It is the girl's father who must seek the boy's people out. That is how it is done in India. Everything is topsy-turvy in our family, thanks to my American sons. Imagine, here we are, parents of the boy, going to meet the girl's father, to beg him to... to do what? "she complained.

"Nothing, my dear, just to meet them and get to know each other. No harm in that! On the other hand you should be proud of the fact that your sons confide in you and seek your help in personal matters. Doesn't that make you happy?" Gopal consoled his wife.

Samir, driving the car, turned and winked at Sandeep who sat on the front seat next to him. "Oh yes, we are good sons, Mom. But then, you are such a sweet mother and have brought us up so well. We must also thank you for having taught the family to bond well."

"Flatterer!" laughed Nimisha, in a better mood now.

Sandeep sat silent through the conversation, lost in worry about how it would all work out. He hoped Ursula's parents would not make it difficult for them and agree to allow them to meet without the necessity of marriage.

The car was about to reach its destination. Guided by the GPS, they were able to locate the given address comfortably. Soon they were driving up the road that led to

Ursula's home. Sandeep looked out eagerly through the window as they swept up a long drive bordered with tall maple trees. Green lawns lay beyond the trees on either side of the road. It soon rounded a bend, to reveal the fine mansion that crowned its end.

"Wow, that's something!" whistled Samir in admiration.

"Rather pretentious, isn't it?" commented Gopal, refusing to be awed by the grandness of the building.

"Look at all the carved pillars and the little balconies. A bit over the top, I think," mumbled Nimisha.

"Well, if you have the means, I guess you can afford the decorations," remarked Samir.

Sandeep was still too nervous to open his mouth. The overwhelming construction that rose before him reminded him of his own shortcomings and the fact that he was not yet fully employed and still partly dependent on his parents. In short, he was no match for the only daughter of an obviously well-off father.

The car swung into the porch. As soon as it halted, the carved doors of the house slid open and an attendant in a navy blue uniform stepped out. He greeted them with a polite bow and a courteous welcome. Then he led them into a large lobby with a gleaming marble floor and dark wood paneling. He took care of their coats and ushered the party into the living room. It was richly decorated with fine Persian carpets, silk curtains and sparkling chandeliers. Making the guests comfortable on the sofas, the man left them to inform his master about their arrival.

Sandeep tapped a foot impatiently on the floor. His brother, guessing that he was nervous, smiled encouragingly at him, "C'mon, relax. Nothing to be tense about, dude!"

"Why should you feel tense? We are the boy's side, after all. Traditional Indian parents feel greatly honored when it is the boy's side that comes to seek a girl's hand. It is the other way around in India!" laughed Gopal.

Just then footsteps were heard outside the door. It was pulled open and a tall, grey haired man in suit and tie stepped into the room, followed by a lady, elegant in her white blouse and long, maroon skirt.

Sandeep's gaze was fixed on the distinguished looking man. He wore a grey well-fitted suit and a matching tie that he recognised as a well-known, expensive brand. To his surprise he saw the gentleman suddenly halt. His brows shot up, as if he was in shock. His eyes grew round in surprise as he stared at the guests. His startled glance darted from Gopal to Nimisha to the two young men who stood before him.

"S...s... sir! M... madam!" the man stammered. "Sa...a... b, you? Sir?"

Astounded, Sandeep stared at him, his mouth open in shock.

"What? What d'you mean, Mr. Pershad?" asked an astonished Gopal. He screwed up his eyes and frowned at the man.

Nimisha was no less surprised. "Have we met before?" she blurted out. She rubbed her eyes, trying to remember if they had indeed met somewhere earlier. Sandeep saw the puzzled frowns on both his parents' faces.

"No, I don't think we have met! I am Mrs. Pershad, Ursula's mother. May I say 'namaste' to you?" Their hostess was the only person who was at ease amongst those present in the room. She had stepped forward and was smiling brightly as she greeted her guests. With her green eyes and pale skin, her black hair touched with grey, she seemed to be an older version of his beloved sweetheart. Sandeep was happy to meet her.

The others, however, looked neither happy nor comfortable. The lines on his father's forehead had deepened, while his mother seemed to be struggling with some unknown emotion he could not understand.

"I don't get it. Who are you? What is your full name? Have we met before? How do you know us?" Gopal asked, sounding a little unhappy at the strange turn of events.

Suddenly Nimisha burst out excitedly, "Oh, now I know! I know who he is!"

At the same time the gentleman, their host, mumbled, "My name... Ram Lakhan Prashad, sir. If you don't mind, sir." He drew back further and seemed to shrink within himself, his head bowed low, as if ashamed of himself.

"Ram... Lakhan?" queried Gopal, still puzzled.

"Ramu! Ramua! Can't you see it's him?" hissed Nimisha into his ears.

"Aha! The servant who ran away from our house! That... that ungrateful chap!" muttered Gopal in a low voice.

Samir jumped to his feet in excitement. "Ramu? You? What a surprise! I remember you, we used to play those computer games together, and I beat you every time. But why did you go away? And where did you vanish?" he asked eagerly.

Ramu did not answer. He kept his head bowed, concentrating on his well-polished shoes. Stunned silence reigned in the room, broken only by the gentle ticking of the clock on the wall.

At last Gopal cleared his throat and said, his voice cold, "So it is you! Ramu! Well, there is nothing further to discuss then. You are a dishonorable man and also undependable. " He stood up, and turned towards the door.

Sandeep looked on, shocked at the strange, unexpected scene that had just unfolded before his eyes. He did not know whether to feel delight or apprehension at the revelation that Ursula's father knew his parents and they too recognized him. He had no idea how and when they had met each other or who Ramu was. He decided to ignore his father's behaviour. In fact he must make up for it, for after all, the scorned gentleman was his beloved's Dad. He could not afford to be rude to him, whatever he may have done to upset his parents.

He stepped forward to shake the gentleman's hand, but found him standing stiff and unmoving, his hands clutching his sides tightly. Ursula's father looked most uncomfortable, while his own parents had turned their faces aside coldly.

Part III :
Ramu and Sandeep

Chapter 22

Mr. Ram Lakhan Prasad

Ramu was shocked to see standing before him the two persons he had no desire to meet again. That life was left behind him long ago; those threads broken once and for all. He was no longer the same humble being who had cooked, washed, cleaned and fetched for others. He had risen far above that position; in fact he knew he was much above, wealth wise, than the poor souls who faced him. After all, he was master of many, whereas they, no doubt, served under other masters. He had a staff of more than fifty while they probably had just a few working under them in some dreary office. He had a white 'phoren' memsahib as wife while they were all just ordinary common people from his own country.

Yes, now he was far superior to those he had bowed before in humility, so why must he cower before them? The thought boosted him, made him raise his head higher, his diffidence gone. He strode towards his favourite seat, the single sofa facing the guests. "Sit, sit down! Let us talk," he said, indicating the empty seats before him.

He noted that Madam, his former 'memsahib' had taken a step towards the door, as if wanting to exit. She returned, with a bewildered expression on her face and seated herself on the sofa he pointed at. Her husband gave her a questioning glance, and sat down beside her. The two youngsters, whom he recognized as the now grown up sons of the couple who sat uneasily on the sofa, joined the rest. In the meantime, his wife was welcoming the guests warmly, smiling at them in a friendly manner.

"Do sit down. I am happy to meet the family my daughter may have a future with. I have heard about you from Ursula. Are you Sandeep?" she inquired, turning towards the young man.

Sandeep nodded, blushing furiously as he shook hands with Ursula's mother. She made him sit beside her, and to make him feel comfortable, laid an arm on his back.

Ramu nodded at Sandeep. "He was a baby at the time, na?" he asked, "So tall he has grown. He is a good match for Ursu. I like him. Good boy! What work you have, boy?"

Sandeep explained that he had finished college and was now undergoing training in an advertising firm. He was yet to settle down.

"And where does big brother work?" Ramu turned to Samir who named the company he was employed with.

"Good jobs, na? Smart boys," remarked Ramu. He still felt shy talking to the two older people and stared at the floor in an embarrassed silence. Fortunately, his wife, who had no reason to be uncomfortable, made polite inquiries about their drive there, while he wondered what to say to his former employers.

The other person quite at ease under the strange situation was Samir. "Tell me, uncle, how did all this happen?" he asked, " I remember you did not know anything about the US. I used to make fun of you because you could not even speak the language! How did you become so rich?" His gaze swept around the room as he raised inquiring eyes to take in the luxurious surroundings.

The admiring expression on the young man's face raised a wave of pride in Ramu's heart. His eyes followed Samir's as the younger man's gaze roved over the various artifacts embellishing the room. "Hard work. And blessings from the One Above," he replied modestly.

Nimisha, who had been sitting there with a frown on her forehead, decided to speak at last. "That does not answer Samir's question, Ramu... er... I mean Mr. Prasad, what brought in this change in your life?"

"Yes, how did you manage all this?" Gopal swept an arm pointedly around, surveying the expensive stuff decorating the room, and glanced at Ramu, "Look at all the stuff here. How is it possible for you to possess all this? May I ask - did you rob a bank or something?" he asked with a smile.

Though the words were said half in jest, Ramu took them seriously. Offended, he sat up straight, face red with indignation. So the man was trying to insult him? Resentment flooded Ramu's mind. He remembered the humiliation of being someone's servant, all the orders he had to meekly obey, the polite 'yes sirs and yes madams' he had to use, the guilt he was made to feel when he made a mistake, the bowing and the scraping to show respect towards those considered to be his masters - the whole idea, in short - of being labeled a 'servant' before beings who thought themselves to be so mighty, so superior.

"So you think I steal all this? You are great, and I am just nobody, someone who must be a servant all his life? I cannot do anything, only sweep and wipe your floors, wash your dirty dishes and cook for you!" declared Ramu hotly, getting up from the sofa, and striding up and down restlessly in the room. "No, no, how can I live in a big house? I must sleep in a corner by your kitchen! Remember that? That's what I did when I first came to your mother's house! That was my place, under your feet!" the memory of the last seemed to agitate him greatly.

Mrs. Prasad rose and rushed to calm him down while Nimisha soothed her husband and scolded him for being rude to the hosts. "It is ok, Ramu. No need to get so furious. We understand you must have worked hard to get here. But do tell us, we are curious, and naturally so, to know your story. The last we knew of you.... you had run away, suddenly, without telling anyone you were leaving. We looked for you everywhere; you must understand how shocked and disturbed we were. So we really want to know. What did you do, where did you work, how did you manage to do so well? That is all. We are curious, you see," she explained.

Ramu soon regained his composure and sank back into his seat, looking more relaxed. He closed his eyes and became thoughtful.

He remembered his old dream of making it big some day, of leading a life such as he had seen in the rare films he had seen back in his village. He remembered with a catch in his breath, the stars that had beckoned him as he lay in his torn blanket on the broken chouki in his father's hut. Yes, even in his shabby clothes, within the mud walls of a hut in a remote village, he had dreamt of a life far, far beyond those walls - and reached for the sky in his imaginations.

And then he had ventured to leave his secure surroundings and dared to flee to the big city. Even there he was not satisfied and had agreed to fly beyond - far, far away to a distant land. Finally he had discarded that sheltered life too, and sought greater riches, adventure and a still better life, for which he had struggled hard and succeeded in finding!

At last he was happy, for he had made his dreams come true. He looked around him at the rich furnishings, the expensive decorations his wife had collected, the carpets and the chandeliers, and at his wife, so stylish and pretty. He remembered the special wall in the room on which hung his photographs with the high and mighty from India; ministers, important politicians, cricketers and film stars, who had dined in his restaurants, famous for their Indian food. His eyes shone with pride and he let out a sigh of satisfaction. Yes, he had made it, he had achieved his aims and here was the final proof of his high status.

The very folk he had served as a lowly servant not very long ago stared at him now with awe and respect as he reclined graciously on his luxurious sofa. Not only this, here was a boy from the family, humbly seeking his daughter's hand. What could be more satisfying than this change in his position?

Ramu raised his head higher. His face had become calm, but his eyes were condescending. He faced the Shuklas squarely, his voice confident.

Chapter 23

Ramu's Story

Yes, he had arrived at last; those dazzling stars so high up and out of reach had been seized and were now in his grasp. The climb to the top had not been easy; but blessed by those very stars; he had succeeded in reaching it. And now here he was, looking down from the skies at those, including his former masters, who were now far below him, on the lower rungs of success.

No doubt the journey had been long and difficult. He remembered those days of struggle when he had laboured hard, perspiration running down his cheeks, in the kitchens and back rooms of restaurants. At times he had wanted to give up, for the heat and the work seemed to be too much, but then he had gritted his teeth and, determined to stay on, had pushed himself harder to achieve more. Days and nights had been filled with the smell of roasting chicken, frying pakoras and sizzling vegetables wrapped in marinates. The tandoor and the oven, the stove and the frying pan, the rolling pin and the chopping board were the stuff his life revolved around. The smell of spices, the smoke from the heating of oils, the fragrance of ghee, lingered always in his nostrils. The continuous demands from customers for the

Punjabi naan and tandoori, the Lucknowi kebabs and the curries, the Hyderabadi biryanis, the Madrasi idli, vadas and dosas, and, the most popular of them all, the Bihari litti chokha still echoed in his ears.

Tired and irritated though he felt with that life, it had given good results. The restaurant flourished, the demanding crowds of visitors led to good profits and before long he had bought out his partner and was the sole owner of a successful eating house. No longer did he have to strive in the kitchen, he had cooks he had trained himself now working under him. Waiters in uniform served the special dishes his restaurant had become famous for, maids washed and cleaned for him, and, best of all, he received great profits. It took several years of running a successful restaurant before he could acquire another. More years and another busy eating place established, then another and another - till a chain of popular Indian restaurants had come up under him, the former cook to an Indian family.

Along the way he had picked up so much - language, manners and the icing on the cake – a beautiful and gracious wife. Irina was the waitress employed at the first restaurant he had owned. Daughter of poor Polish immigrants who were now American citizens, she had soon caught his attention by the deference she displayed towards him, the feeling she gave him of acknowledging him as her boss and superior. And showing he was someone to be respected even though his skin was so brown or 'kaala' in comparison to her own alabaster white body. He, too, had found himself drawing closer to her.

Ramu glanced at the confident woman smiling back at him and sighed with gratitude. It was only because of her that he had been able to remain there in the land of his dreams. For quite some time he had stayed only in the kitchens and the backrooms of the restaurants where he had worked, hidden from view, scared and nervous that he may be found out, someone without the permission to live in the country. But then Irina had come into his life. It was because of her that he had been able to acquire US citizenship. Married to an American citizen, he had succeeded in staying on.

Were there any regrets? Yes, there were. Left far behind in his long journey was the girl he had loved in his youth, the mischievous Urmi, the aspiring artist he had promised to help. He had let her down – how could he forgive himself for it? But then in life you had to give up something to get more and he had found happiness with Irina, the other person who had come into his life.

He had to do it, had to give up his first love. For far too long he had kept promising – yes, wait, he would come and fetch her, as soon as he had made some money. He would come soon, but slowly, as days passed and he was unable to send for her, she had perhaps understood. And then came her letter releasing him from the bonds that may have existed between the two, and from all expectations from him.

She had taken a decision, and she hoped he would understand, she had written. No, it was not her family, for they had long ago given up the idea of fixing a groom for her and had allowed her to lead her life the way she wanted.

And she had made the most of it. "I went to high school, cycling all the way to the next village. You know the government here has given us girls these cycles. They wanted us to study, you see. I made the most of it. And then I met this man. He is so much my senior. He came to our village to see the wall paintings he had heard about from someone. And when he saw the paintings I had done he really liked them. He became a friend and told me he wanted to show my work to others. And now he has brought me here, to the big city of Mumbai. He has introduced me to important people, who promote folk art. They organize displays of our Sohrai art in the country as well as abroad.

And now he has asked me to marry him, and I have gladly agreed. We can travel together now, and are to hold exhibitions in far off countries. I feel so excited to be travelling with him. We are to go to strange places. You may not even have heard of them, like Vienna, Rome, and…. Oh, but I forget which others! It is all so exciting for me!"

Ramu felt happy to hear that she had succeeded in fulfilling her ambition of achieving success as an artist. It made him feel better. Whatever feeling of guilt he had felt about not doing anything for her had been assuaged by news of her achievement.

The thoughts raced across his mind as Ramu tried to answer the questions asked by the visitors. His reply, however, was brief as he looked thoughtfully back at them. "I worked hard, very, very hard. I am good cook. I thank Badi Ma'am, who taught me so, so much. First, I worked in a hotel. 'Litti chokha' was my special dish. People loved my 'litti chokha'. Soon, from cook I became owner!" he said proudly, "First one, then one more, I opened many hotels, slowly and slowly. People liked my hotel food. So they came. They still come. And she," he turned to his wife, "Irina helped me. I thank her with all my heart."

"No, no, it is all his talent and hard work!" protested Irina, with a laugh, "I was only good at spending what he earned!"

"She spent well. She decorated my hotels. She spent cleverly and so we have this house now," Ramu gave his wife a grateful and admiring glance, "She is a good wife. Yes, a very good wife!"

Nimisha and Gopal had listened to Ramu with patience, but with glum expressions. Ramu waited now to hear them mention his beloved daughter. "Dad," Ursula had shyly informed them, "They will come to talk to you about their son and me and seek your permission. Be nice to them, please. We really love each other!"

There was no such mention. Instead he was shocked when Gopal suddenly shot up from his seat. "It is late now. We have to go far," he muttered, "Thank you for welcoming us, but we must leave now." Nimisha stared at her husband for a moment before following him to the door.

"B...but, Sir, you were going to say something?" reminded Ramu, puzzled.

"That's Ok. Some other time," Gopal threw back the words at him before walking out of the room, followed by his wife.

"Papa, hey, what about us? Wait!" Samir shouted after him. Sandeep was too astounded to utter a word. The two young men, shocked at their parents' rude behavior, glanced apologetically at their host and hesitated a few seconds before finally deciding to follow their elders out of the house.

Ramu stared at the vanishing backs with a bewildered expression. "Arre, what... where... but why are you going?" he muttered.

"They did not even touch the tea," murmured Irina, just as puzzled. Ramu could only shake his head in shock.

Chapter 24

Sandeep's Questions

"But why, Papa? Why did you rush out so rudely?" asked Samir once they were back in their car and driving out through the gates of the mansion.

"You did not say a word about Ursula and me. You forgot what you came for," accused Sandeep.

"I know the reason, of course!" said Nimisha. She turned to her husband, "But you do the explaining."

"What is there to explain? How can we even <u>think</u> of marrying our son into that man's family? Totally out of question. I don't even want to discuss it," said Gopal.

"Please understand, Sandeep. Your father is right. After all, there has to be something in common between the two families. Now that you know the background, I am sure you will also change your mind about being friends with that girl," explained Nimisha.

"What's wrong with them?" Sandeep's voice was puzzled, and edged with rising anger. He did not want to quarrel with his parents over a girl but he could not understand the unfair prejudice they felt against Ursula's family.

"Everybody is equal in the USA," asserted Sameer, coming to his brother's rescue. "Our parents are a little shocked, brother, but give them some time and I am sure they will come around and agree. Patience, dude."

"But why? I just don't understand. It...it is not fair. I love Ursula. I...I cannot live without her. And what is wrong with them? Perfectly decent people, rich home...better than ours, let me tell you. Then...then...why, WHY?" he burst out with passion.

"Hush, dear, calm yourself," Nimisha tried to comfort her disappointed, furious son, "We know you are upset. But we will find someone even better and more suited to our family. There are plenty of pretty girls we know...."

"NO! I do not want anyone else. I love her and I have promised her. There cannot be anyone else... how can you even say that there can be another person? How can you, Mom?" His voice broke into an anguished, desperate sob.

Gopal remained unmoved. Nimisha leaned over to stroke her son's arm in a vain attempt to comfort him. He shook off her arm and moved off to distance himself from the elders on the back seat. An uneasy silence settled over the occupants of the car as it hurtled along the highway. Samir concentrated on the steering wheel, thus avoiding being drawn into the controversy. He drove fast towards New York and home, wishing to get over the unpleasant situation as soon as he possibly could. It was getting dark now and this only deepened the gloom that had descended on the passengers in the car.

Sandeep's mind raced as fast as did the car speeding past the milestones on the highway. Why did his parents reject Ursula's family? He had understood by now that her father was the man who had disappeared from their home many years ago, an incident he had only heard about from various members of his family, after he was old enough to comprehend adult talk. But how did it matter now? He probably had his own reasons to leave; the very fact that he had made good in life and reached somewhere showed that he was not only ambitious but also intelligent enough to achieve his dreams. Why should it go against him? Everyone had the right to aspire, to dream of bigger things and try to achieve their aims. Did not his father, brother, and even his mother have ambitions and aimed high? So why must Mr. Prasad be despised for doing it? How could his parents disregard their son's feelings and so summarily reject the person he loved so madly?

And - he was doubly certain by now - he would eventually marry.

The sudden ringing of Sandeep's phone pierced the tense silence that lay heavy in the car, startling its occupants. "Your phone!" said Samir, "Why don't you pick it up?"

Sandeep had already glanced at the information on the phone and knew it was Ursula who was trying to reach him. He was in no mood to talk to her and quickly switched off the phone. What was the point? She was sure to be curious about their meeting with her parents. On the other hand if her parents had already spoken to her she would have known what had happened and was probably angry with him and his family for walking off, that too without any explanation. What would he say? What explanation could he give for their strange behavior? No, he did not wish to speak to her just now. Maybe later, when he was face to face with her.

The phone rang again. "It is Ursula. What do you want me to say to her?" He turned around and looked accusingly at his mother. "Now that you have messed up my life what do you want me to do?"

"Simple. Switch it off, dude!" advised Samir.

Sandeep had already done so, but he had not bargained for Ursula's persistence. It was Samir's phone that rang this time. Of course, he should have remembered. He had given his brother's number to her himself, so that she could contact him about arranging a meeting between their parents.

"Can't talk. I am driving. Guess its best that you speak to Ursula. Tell her you will explain it all later," suggested Samir, pointing to the phone that lay on his lap.

He was right. Poor girl, she must be so worried, so anxious to know what had happened. He had to speak to her. He picked up the still ringing instrument and pressed the button.

"Hello. Is it Samir Shukla?"

"Ursula, this is Sandeep. Sorry I could not talk earlier...."

"Oh! What happened, Sandeep? My mother said you left, suddenly, for no reason at all... she did not know.... Shocking! But why?"

"Can I speak to you later? We are driving home. Everybody is listening... I will explain when we meet... let's talk later. Can you wait? Love you," Sandeep spoke in as low a voice as possible and switching it off, handed the phone back to his brother.

"We are sorry about this, Sandeep. But you must understand..." began his mother. She reached out to pat his shoulder, in her attempt once again to comfort her son.

Sandeep shook off the hand and shifted position. He maintained a stubborn silence that spoke more than any words could have done. The resentment in his heart grew deeper. The desire uppermost in his mind was to open the door and jump out of the car but he restrained himself with great effort. The tension between the four deepened further, as each struggled to deal with the thoughts that disturbed each of them.

They were soon nearing their destination. Now there were more cars whizzing by on the highway, making Samir sit straight and alert, his attention fixed on the signboards they passed. Sandeep, on the other hand, sank deeper and deeper into a morass of despair as he remembered that at the end of the journey he would have to face Ursula and answer her questions. What was he to tell her? How was he to explain his parents' strange behavior to someone who had grown up in America where, everyone, supposedly, was considered to be socially equal?

No, his parents would have to answer the question. What was wrong with the girl's father, now that he had risen in life and reached a respectable status and position? Why did they still persist with their unreasonable prejudice?

At last he had made up his mind. He turned around to find his mother's gaze fixed questioningly on him. His father looked more relaxed. In fact his eyes were closed. He seemed to have dozed off.

"What is it, beta?" asked Nimisha gently, seeing the wild look in her son's eyes. "I know you are angry, but...?"

"I just don't understand. If he is a different person now, why are you both against him? Why?" Sandeep almost shouted.

The anger in his voice made Gopal open his eyes and lean forward with the stern expression he used when he wanted to scold his boys for some mischief they had committed. Sandeep remembered how that glance used to fill him with a feeling of guilt and make him say sorry, even when he felt he had done no wrong. But no, he was not going to succumb this time, for he certainly had every right to fight for the sake of the girl he loved.

"But why, Dad?" he asked in a voice that was low, though still firm and demanding, "There has to be a good reason, and you have to convince me about it."

"Alright, I will tell you why. He was a SERVANT in our house and Nani's! Now do you understand? How can you marry a servant's daughter? We are a respectable Indian family. We cannot have a servant's daughter as a member of our family! You want people to laugh at us? Forget it! Just forget it!" Gopal's voice was loud and decisive.

It was an order, in fact, as Sandeep well knew. Though he still did not understand why his parents were so dead against it, he decided not to question them any further. There was no point, and anyway, the car had already entered deep into the city. They would soon be home.

Ursula would be waiting. He must talk to her before he went a step further.

What would be her reaction?

Chapter 25

Ramu is Ready to Fight

Ramu stared, aghast, at the backs of the departing visitors. No explanations, no apologies – they had just walked out of his house. What did it mean? Puzzled though he was, deep within himself he perhaps understood enough to feel a growing sense of rejection. Yes. That is what it was. They had spurned not just him, his home and wife, but - and it was this that hurt the most – also his beloved daughter. His beautiful, talented, well-educated, college-going daughter, who was, in his eyes, the embodiment of all that was perfect, was of no consequence to them. Along with her parents, she too had received the boot from someone who considered himself to be the lord and master of the universe, thought the embittered Ramu. He glanced around at the expensive stuff his wife had furnished his home with and sighed deeply. No use. The luxuries did not matter. What he was once, years ago, was actually the reality. There was no escaping it. In the eyes of those who knew him then, he was still the same slave, the low caste, humble 'chhokra' meant to clean and sweep and look after the needs of the high and mighty. He had no right to dream big, no right to strive towards a better life, no right to live well in a big house.

After all, he was just a servant. How could he aspire to wed his daughter to a boy from a different class altogether?

"I think you have understood those people's action. You have guessed why they left so suddenly, haven't you?" Irina laid a gentle hand on her husband's shoulder, "It is still a mystery to me. But your face tells me that you know. Won't you tell me, your wife?"

"Bad people. They left because I was once poor," muttered Ramu.

"So what? Now you are not poor. I am sure you have a better home than those Indians."

"That does not matter. I worked in their house. I was a 'naukar', a servant. My job is to **serve** - to do all the dirty work, to wash, clean and cook for the 'malik', the master. Still they think that. Now also. But I am not the same man now," Ramu sighed and buried his face in his hands.

"I did the same work in your restaurant. But it was so long ago. We have risen to a higher status now. There are others to do the job for us, so it should be okay now. It should not matter any more," Irina bent and pulled Ramu's hands away from his face, and met the troubled eyes of her husband. "Come on, cheer up. I don't like it when you are sad."

"People in India are like that only," grumbled Ramu. "They don't care what you are now. They only see the old days, the old you."

Irina stroked Ramu's hair and murmured soothing words to make him feel better. "They did not eat, but never mind. Let us have our dinner. Come, you must be hungry."

Just then the phone rang. It was Ursula, impatient to find out how the visit had gone. "Hi Papa. Did you like them? What did you think of Sandeep?" Her chirpy voice rang out, loud enough for both to hear. Ramu handed the phone to Irina. "You tell," he muttered gloomily.

"Hello, Baby, how are you?" Irina tried to sound cheerful.

"Never mind how I am!" laughed the voice at the other end, "I am excited about the visit. Wasn't Sandeep handsome? How were his people? Did Papa like them?"

Slowly, trying to be as gentle as possible, Irina related the day's events. For a long time there was no response from the girl. "But...but why?" came the soft gasp a few moments later. "Alright, do not worry. I will speak to Sandeep," she said as she quickly disconnected her mobile..

Questions hung in the air but neither of the two voiced them. Ramu did not want to eat and refused to be coaxed into having a bite. Irina ate a few morsels and ordered the butler to remove the food tray. She knew her husband was in no mood to eat and she did not want to irritate him by insisting on it. She well understood his disappointment and thought it wiser to stay silent.

It was some time before the shrill ringing of the phone roused the two from their apathy. Ramu picked up the phone and his face lit up when he heard his daughter's voice at the other end. "Don't worry, Dad. I have spoken to

Sandeep. He did not say much as he was with the family on the drive home, but we will talk about it when we meet. I am sure all will be fine; he will explain it all. You guys do not worry, alright?"

The poor girl was still cheerful and Ramu did not want to spoil it by letting her know his feelings. Maybe she was right. Maybe there was some other explanation that had nothing to do with his earlier life; he had just come to a hasty conclusion because he still felt inferior before his previous bosses. With an effort he pulled himself up and smiled at Irina. "Alright. Let's not think about it. Let's have dinner."

Relieved to see the cloud lift from Ramu's face Irina quickly sent for a light meal for her husband who had refused it earlier. The two retired to bed soon after and tried to sleep off their worries.

It was not that easy. Ramu tossed and turned in bed. What would happen if 'that family' forbade their son from meeting his daughter? It would be such a blow to his daughter's happiness, for she had confessed to her parents that she had fallen madly in love with Sandeep. He could not bear to see his daughter unhappy. No, no, how could he allow them to do this to his little girl? He would fight them tooth and nail if they caused his daughter any grief, he would go to the police; he would kidnap the boy.... He would go to any length to see that his daughter was happy. With this resolve in mind, Ramu finally fell into restless slumber.

The thoughts, however, pursued him relentlessly throughout the long night and forced him awake as soon as dawn broke. Irina was fast asleep next to him but was soon awake, disturbed by her husband's restless movements in their bedroom.

"No, no, will not allow! 'That family' cannot destroy my 'pyari beti'! They cannot! They... they sleep at night in same room! Yes. They stay in one room... my friend, he said. So? And his people go away, no talk about wedding! What do they think? She is cheap bazaar girl? She is that boy's slave, she is...no...no, I cannot even speak that dirty word? They think she is my girl, so she is a slave, a no good maid?" Ramu was muttering, walking up and down restlessly in the bedroom.

"Stop it. You don't know the real reason. You are just imagining the worst. Wait till Ursula has talked to the boy and found out what happened," Irina argued, now fully awake.

"I will kill him if he makes her sad. I will send the boy to jail. He cannot sleep with her, then leave her...," continued Ramu, ignoring her advice. He was already dressed up and ready to rush out of the house.

"Where are you going? At this time of the day?" Irina asked, surprised to see him preparing to leave.

"I know 'that family's' house. They can still be there. I am going to Chicago. To shout... and ask them... will your son marry my girl? If no, I will....I will ... just wait... see what I will do!" Ramu almost yelled.

"No, you can't do that! Without knowing the details, how can you just go and fight?"

Irina caught Ramu's arm and held it hard. Her husband tried to shake her off. But she clutched him tighter with both her hands and would not let him go. It took her a long time and all her strength and power of persuasion to prevent him from rushing to confront 'that family.'

Chapter 26

Sandeep and Ursula

On return to New York, Sandeep bid goodbye to his family calmly enough, though inwardly he was seething with resentment and anger. It was time now to face the unpleasant. He decided to meet Ursula as quickly as possible. It would be a very difficult situation but she must be waiting anxiously to hear from him. Though it was late night she would be too worried to fall asleep, he well knew.

He was right. The phone was picked up the moment it was connected to hers. "Sandeep? At last! I have been waiting... you cannot imagine how impatiently! Are you back?"

"Yes," replied Sandeep, "Where are you? In your room?"

"Where else? What happened?"

"Look, can we meet? Is it too late for me to come and see you!" was the hurried reply. Sandeep did not want to give the shocking news on the phone. It had to be done when they were together.

"Come on, I can take it, whatever it is. I have waited too long. Cannot bear it any more. Sandeep, you have to tell me what happened. Why did they leave without saying anything? Why?"

"Not on the phone; I am coming over to meet you just now, unless you want to sleep," insisted Sandeep.

"How can you expect me to sleep? Come right over. I can't wait to see you," replied Ursula.

As he walked down the familiar lane under the dark shadows of the branches above, Sandeep felt the numbness that had settled over him, ever since his parents had rejected his girl, slowly melt away. About to meet her at last, the numbness was replaced by the feeling of shock that now gripped his heart. His steps became heavy and slowed down. Somehow he forced himself to walk on until he finally stood outside her door. He lifted a heavy hand to press the bell.

The door was opened immediately. The flushed, tense face of Ursula lit up with an expectant smile. "Oh, Sandeep. Missed you so much! So happy to see you again!" And then she was in his arms, kissing his cheeks and lips and pressing herself tight against him. They remained thus for a few moments until she finally drew back a few steps. "Alright. Now tell me what happened. Why did they go away so suddenly?"

"The...the...the...they...do not approve," stammered Sandeep, grief and embarrassment thickening his voice; his face had turned red, his eyes evaded hers.

"So what's wrong with me?" demanded Ursula, her voice aggressive.

"Not w...with you. It is Mr. P... Pershad, your father," stammered Sandeep.

"Well, you and your parents are...excuse me...as Indian and brown as him. If that is their objection ... I don't see any difference between my father and them," the words were sarcastic and accusing. She drew further away from him.

Sandeep hung his face down and remained quiet.

"So?" demanded Ursula, "Have you nothing to say?"

"I am sorry. Sorry, baby. It is not about the colour of the skin... they have another reason which I find difficult to explain... I don't know how to tell you..." His eyes, though, had much to say, while the downturned lips revealed the misery in his heart.

"You better tell me," Ursula's voice softened at the sight, "I can take it, love." She definitely sounded gentler now for her heart had melted to see Sandeep look so downcast. She reached out suddenly to touch his cheek. She stroked his face, her gaze caressing him as her voice made soothing sounds full of love. "Don't worry, my sweet. We'll handle it together, whatever it is. We'll change your parents' opinion about our family, whatever their objections might be. But please...please, don't hide it from me. Tell me, and we'll work it out together," she was murmuring.

Greatly relieved and reassured, Sandeep clasped her close and held her against him for a long time. "Alright. Let me tell you," he said finally, drawing a deep breath of determination, "You see, it turned out that your father was a house help to my parents years and years ago. I was a baby then, but I had heard that he had suddenly vanished one day, without informing them that he was going away."

"Well, that is not such a tragedy, is it? He went away because he aspired to do better in life. What's wrong with that? Did you see our home? Does it look any worse than anyone else's? He managed to do so well. I am proud of my father. He struggled and achieved so much in his life. He is equal to anyone now," argued Ursula.

"Yes. The house definitely was a rich man's home! I was certainly impressed. But obviously my parents were not," Sandeep gave a wry smile, "Their admiration vanished when they met the owner of the place and recognized him."

"But why? I still don't understand."

"I asked the same question. When he has changed and become like any of us, why should they reject him?"

"So?"

"It was my father who finally replied – 'He is … was, a **servant!** How can we have a **servant's** daughter as family?' And that was his objection to our being together."

The seconds ticked by in painful silence. Sandeep could see that Ursula was too stunned to react to the shock he seemed to have given her. He stretched out his hand to comfort her but she pushed it off and turned her face away.

"You must understand that I do not agree with him at all. I do not believe in any kind of inequality…," he hastened to say.

In a flash Ursula had twisted around to face him. "You'd better not! I cannot believe that anyone in today's world can even think of such things! Servant! What do they mean by this? This is not ancient times that you consider a person to be a servant! My mother was also someone helping in a hotel. But she was not condemned as a *servant!*"

Sandeep had no answer. A painful silence followed, broken suddenly by Ursula's sharp query, "And what about me? Am I a servant too? A maid… or a house help? What am I?"

"You are a college student and my beloved," mumbled Sandeep.

"Well… thanks. Glad to know that you take me to be a student, and not a servant," her tone had turned sarcastic once again. The next moment her voice became contrite and she touched his arm lightly. "Oh, sorry. Did not want to hurt you, but I do feel angry. Here we are, talking all the time about equality, and the freedom to be and do what one wants, and then to hear people expressing such silly, prejudiced thoughts really maddens me. You must tell them, Sandeep. They are just being outrageously prejudiced and old -fashioned."

"I agree with you whole-heartedly, you do not have to convince me about it. But we must now decide what we must do…," began Sandeep when Ursula suddenly interrupted him.

"Oh no! I forgot… must ring up home and speak to them! They were so upset. They don't know why your people just walked away. Must tell them… but, what shall I say? They will be so hurt... !" Her face twisted suddenly with pain and her eyes brimmed over with tears. She hid her face in both her hands. Her voice was anguished and her words unclear as she cried out, "What shall I tell them, Sandeep? What can I say? I cannot... do not want to hurt my Dad!"

Sandeep stood awkwardly silent. He was as upset as she was, and could not find any words to console her.

"Go now! Let me think... its no use your standing here. Let me ... just go, Sandeep!" insisted Ursula turning her back on her friend and running towards her room. He heard the door being banged shut.

He knew there was nothing that he could do, at least until she had recovered from the shock.

Chapter 27

Angela's Anger

Sandeep remained in a daze the next day as well. He wanted to rush to Ursula's place to find out if she had spoken to her parents. He wanted to know how her father had responded to her explanation – whether he was angry, or sad or what? He wanted to hug her close to his heart and kiss her, he wanted to shout at his own parents and ... he wanted to defy them and run away somewhere with the girl he loved. Who cared about what people said? He certainly did not. It was his life, his girl's and his. It had nothing to do with anyone else. How did it matter to anyone how the two young persons led their lives - and so on - raced his jumbled thoughts.

But soon enough, he realized that he did hunger for his parents' approval of the choice he had made. He wanted those closest to him to like and love his girl, just as he did. He wanted his mother to appreciate the person he had chosen to live with, his grandmother to continue to look at her with that gleam of admiration, just as she had done when she had first met her at his brother's wedding. And, now, most of all, he wanted his father to respect the parents of the girl he intended to spend his life with, irrespective of what had happened in the past.

He was impatient now to hear from Ursula. What was her father's reaction on hearing the reason for his parents' hasty departure from the scene? What exactly did she tell them? He hoped they did not take it too badly, for that would be the end of his relationship with Ursula. She would be too angry to meet him. As the hours passed without any news from her, Sandeep could not bear it any more. At last he picked up his mobile and clicked the numbers on it.

The phone was switched off. No response. His growing anxiety and desperation finally forced him to leave his work and hasten once again to meet Ursula. She was not in college. Her friends informed him that she had not come to class that day. Where was she then? He rushed to the girls' hostel but she was not in her rooms either.

Alarmed now, Sandeep turned to his phone again. 'Where are you? Very worried. Please respond', he messaged her. But the instrument remained unresponsive and indifferent. Quite at his wit's end he turned his steps back towards his workplace. He had just walked past the hostel gates when his eyes fell on the girl he recognized as Ursula's friend, Angela Brown. He had not seen her for a long time and it took him a few moments to remember where and how he had met her.

Before he could greet her, Angela had herself turned towards him, a frown on her face. "Hi, I'm so glad to see you. But what have you done to my friend?" she asked before he could open his mouth, "I have never seen her so disturbed."

"Where is she? I have been looking for her. She is neither at college nor in the dorm. Do you know where she is?"

"I do know. Let's sit down somewhere where we can talk. Shall we?"

It was the same coffee shop where he had first met Ursula, remembered Sandeep as he entered the crowded room once again. Impatient and anxious, he followed Angela to a more secluded area where they could converse comfortably. As soon as the coffee had been ordered he turned to her. "Ok, tell me now! How is she, and where?"

"She has rushed home. Said she wanted to be with her father when she tells him what you said. He will be so shocked... she said... it is so wrong of your people," Angela's voice turned indignant as she added, "How could they...you... hurt them so much!"

"So you know?" Sandeep asked.

"Of course I do! I am her friend. She confided in me. I am as angry and shocked as she was. To turn away so rudely and leave without a word of explanation... and then to say that he was...was... not their equal, just because he was a domestic worker years ago! So what if he was? Weren't *my* people slaves... at one time long ago? In fact our family came up North only a generation ago. So should we be considered untouchable today? Of course not! How dare anyone say she cannot be accepted by the family, just because she is the daughter of someone who helped in their house?"

"I agree. I did not like it myself," Sandeep looked shamefaced as he hastened to clarify his position.

Angela continued to glare at him indignantly. "Just like you Indians! You continue with your silly prejudices, beliefs you have not given up even after centuries have passed and the world has changed. Man, you are in the US now, not in your caste ridden, ignorant, illiberal country! Shed those feelings of superiority, you are part now of a society which is trying to promote equality, man! Colour and class should not matter any more. Don't you understand?" Proudly, she stretched out a bare arm and stroked her dark skin, as if to remind him of her own different colour. "See! Brown, black or white! Does it matter? No, it should not! But I know it does in your country! In India! That day you gave a long lecture on gender equality and against all forms of discrimination! But you do not seem to believe in what you preach to others. Shame on you!"

Her vitriol filled words forced Sandeep to protest just as strongly. "Stop blaming me. I am as liberal as anyone else here. And I believe in what I said at that meeting. Anyway, it is not a question of colour; it is something quite different. It is a matter of class! Though let me tell you, I do not at all agree with my parents!"

"Then go and tell them to apologise! How could they even mention the word 'servant' with reference to my friend's father? Is he a mere 'servant' to them, after he has achieved so much in life? What he has achieved and the struggle he went through in reaching where he has, is superior to anything your father has done in his life. No wonder my friend is so upset!"

"I do understand. But tell me... what do you think I must do now?" Sandeep, on the defensive now after the onslaught of words from Angela, thought it best to mollify her by seeking her advice.

"Tell them they are wrong. That they have no right to foist such outdated ideas on their son and his dear friend. Tell them they must meet Mr. Pershad and apologise for their disgusting behavior," ordered Angela, her voice heated.

"You may be right. But I don't know if they will agree. My father was quite categorical about it. 'Out of the question' he told me. It will need some persuasion from me and even then...," he ended tamely on a doubtful note.

"Well then, my friend will have no other option. She will break her relationship with you. It will be painful, but what else can she do? Surely you do not expect her to continue meeting someone whose family has no respect for her people?"

"But we love each other very much. I know she does too. Perhaps...," Sandeep began when she cut in with a snort.

"Hah! That's what you think. But I could see where her loyalty lay. She told me, in fact, that she was really concerned about her father. She could not hurt him. No, she does not want to hurt him! Whatever it may cost her!" she repeated emphatically.

"Alright. Thanks for telling me," said Sandeep, after a long and tense pause. "Let me think about it. I must leave now. Thanks once again. Goodbye."

Pushing back his chair, he rose, paid the bill at the counter and without a backward look strode out of the room where he had earlier spent so many delightful coffee and chat sessions with Ursula.

By evening Sandeep was so agitated that he made up his mind to rebel against his parents. He grew more and more restless as the hours passed and he failed to contact Ursula. Finally he decided to speak to his brother and seek his advice.

Samir was sympathetic, but at the same time more concerned about his parents' feelings.

"I can imagine how shocked they must have been to see Ramu there!" Sandeep was amazed to hear his brother's reply. He could detect a distinct hint of a smile in Samir's voice, which, however, he decided to ignore. "Just think, they had known him as a humble simpleton running their errands and serving them at table. I remember him well. I used to laugh at his ignorance. He was so stupid, and lost all the games I made him play! And there he was that day - all suited -booted, pretending to be a real gentleman! Living in a big house, a stylish lady by his side! Not only that - a butler to serve *him*, who was himself less than a butler not long ago! Ha, Ha! No wonder they were so shocked!"

Sandeep definitely did not like it. But as it was no use protesting, he refrained from answering back.

"Don't worry, dude," Samir tried to console him, "I am sure you will find a better match soon. In any case you are not about to get married, at least not until you are well settled in a good job. No, I am not telling you to forget

Ursula; you may continue with her as before. Who knows? By the time you are ready to settle down and get married, you may well meet someone else and change your mind about her? It happens. So don't get so upset. Just enjoy life with her, for the present."

It was certainly not what Sandeep wanted to hear. He was sure Ursula was the girl for him and he definitely was not going to change his mind about her. How could his brother even suggest such an impossible idea? Disappointed and miserable, he at last decided to go to Chicago and meet his parents. He must convince them that she was the only one he would marry and they had better shed their prejudices and accept her.

Chapter 28

Ramu and his Daughter

"Mom, Dad, I am home!"

Somehow Irina had succeeded in calming Ramu. It was afternoon, and the couple sat in the comfortable family room, watching their favorite TV show, when they heard a car drive in, followed by the opening and shutting of doors. Light steps outside told them they had a visitor. Irina turned to her husband excitedly and cried, "Hey, that sounds like someone we know!" The next moment the door burst open and there stood their daughter, an uncertain smile on her lips, and a strange look in her eyes.

"Ursu!" cried Ramu, "You are here?" His eyes had lit up on seeing his beloved daughter, but darkened when he noticed the paleness of her cheeks. "What is it, beta, are you ok?"

"I am so sorry, Dad... I... I am so angry with them! They should not have gone away like that...!" Ursula ran to her mother and put her arms around her. Ramu felt his eyes well up as he watched mother and daughter hug each other. He stretched out his arms and drew them both towards him. The three stood close together for some time before Irina straightened herself and moved towards a chair. "Come, sit down, both of you. Let's relax. Coffee, everyone?"

The other two nodded and Irina rang the bell to order snacks and coffee for the family. "Alright, Ursu. Now tell us, what happened and why did they leave so suddenly. Your father was so upset. He made up all kinds of disturbing explanations, of his past life, and so on. Did you talk to your boyfriend?"

Ramu tried to guess what was coming. The boy had broken his relationship with his daughter. That was the reason behind her pale face and the tearful eyes. He gripped the arms of his chair and gritted his teeth as he waited for her to reply. He could see how disturbed the poor girl was. Waves of anger swept across his heart as he watched the expressions that flitted across her sweet, tender face. He turned his gaze away from her to frown at the expensive carpets that covered the floors of the room. What use were they, when they had failed to impress his former masters?

"I did," Ursula spoke at last, in a low, trembling voice, "His parents were ... did not like ... the fact that Dad had once worked for them."

"Is that all? What does your friend think?" Irina asked, "It does not matter what they feel. What does *he* think? Is he alright with this fact?"

"It is perfectly fine with him!" Ursula's voice sounded more cheerful, Ramu was relieved to see. But he felt parents' approval was just as important, specially if they were from his own country, India, where elders were respected and generally obeyed by sons and daughters.

"Well, if it is alright with him, that should be okay for us. Cheer up, baby. You do not have to look so sad. You are friends with the son, not the parents!" Irina smiled at her daughter. Relief was writ large on her face.

Ursula glanced at her father. Ramu was shaking his head disapprovingly. "Happy to hear, beta. So that boy did not hurt my girl. I will bash him up if he hurts you. But we want his mother – father to like you also. You cannot be happy in family that will not like you. Families, too, must love the girl, no, Irina?"

Irina nodded in agreement. "So what is their problem? Why are they against us? What is wrong with us?" she wondered.

"How can we marry our son to our servant's daughter? That is what they told Sandeep!" explained Ursula, her voice low and bitter.

"That is really silly. He is not a servant any more. Does he look like one?" Irina muttered angrily, "How dare they say such things against my husband?"

"And what do they mean by such horrible comments? *Servant* – what's that? No one uses that term, in any case. It's disgusting – how dare they call my father such names? I...I hate them!" cried Ursula passionately.

Ramu listened to them in silence, his heart full of conflicting emotions. That term again! His mind went back to that day years ago, when he was told that he was wanted to work in a family in Delhi, as a servant. He remembered how indignant he had felt. He was not a servant; he was heir to a piece of land, however small; he was a farmer's son, though poor, no doubt; and he was ready to take up any job he could find, however humble. Did this make him someone not to be respected as another human being? A person to be spurned, to be kept under one's feet and treated as a pariah! Anger rose in his heart. Just because he was ready to take up work that some people disdained he was forever branded as a lower human being. Instead of respecting a person's work and feeling grateful to him for his help, he was looked at with suspicion and distanced socially. Not fair, his mind screamed.

The next moment he hung his head down as a feeling of shame descended on him. Of course, how could he equate himself with those who were so well educated and earned so much more than him who had not studied further than the eighth in a remote village school? It was not surprising at all that the educated and the cultured rich spurned him. Yes, he was definitely inferior to them and it was time he accepted the fact. However far he had reached in his new life in a country other than his own, he would forever remain a lower human being in the eyes of the educated and the privileged. His head sank lower and he closed his eyes with a sigh. His daughter was doomed; she would forever remain a servant's kin for the family of the man she loved.

"NO!" He burst out. He would not allow it. They had brought her up well. He had seen to it that she went to a good school; she was not in any way inferior to any other girl in the US. Irina had made sure that she had grown up to be a lady who could fit in any society. So what if he was still a rough, half educated villager; his daughter was a smart college student.

"No, beti!" Ramu patted his daughter's shoulder and tried to comfort her. "No, don't marry that boy. No, if parents don't want, you should not. I will find someone for you. A good boy with good job! You forget him, ok? I know many good boys. Don't worry, ok?"

"How can you say that, Papa?" interrupted Ursula, "How can I think of someone else? I love him! I do not want anyone else! I... I... cannot!" She hid her face in her hands and burst into tears.

"It is ok, baby, we understand. Don't cry. We will think of something," Irina put her arms around her daughter and tried to comfort her with soft, soothing murmurs of affection.

Pain and bitterness filled his heart as Ramu watched the two. It was a situation he did not know how to deal with, he realized. He felt useless and helpless, a parent who had let his daughter down by being born into a poor, unsophisticated, rural household.

However well educated and cultured his daughter may become, she would forever be linked to him, specially in the eyes of those who had known him as a lowly servant, an illiterate, uncouth villager meant to remain under the boots of his masters.

Chapter 29

Sandeep in Chicago

It would be difficult to convince his parents but Sandeep knew he had to do it. He caught the train to Chicago and hired a taxi to take him to his home in the suburbs. The taxi took a long time to reach, caught as it was in the traffic jams that often besieged the city.

It was almost evening by the time he finally rang the bell and waited for the door to open. He heard the slow, heavy footsteps and knew it was his grandmother who would be the first to greet him. He was right. The door opened to reveal his Nani, Mrs. Misra. Sandeep smiled uncertainly at her wondering if she knew about Ursula and her parents.

"What a pleasant surprise!" cried his grandmother, beaming with delight, "Come, come in, dear boy! Your parents are not back from work, but never mind, I am here... so happy to see you. Tell me, how did you come? Hope all is fine with you. But let me welcome you first, I will make you some coffee... and there are plenty of your favourite cookies to go with it. Do make yourself comfortable first. Go unpack, while I get the coffee ready... !" she bustled around busily while he walked to his old familiar room upstairs to dump his bag as well as himself on the bed.

Ah, the old well-loved pictures on the walls, the cozy bed he had snuggled in every night in the past, the welcome smell of coffee wafting up from the kitchen below – it was good to be back in his old familiar surroundings. He relaxed with a sigh and threw himself on his bed. For a few moments he forgot his troubles as his mind flew back to his childhood. Memories of his parents giving in to his demands and pampering him flashed before his eyes. They were sure to treat him with the same love and care again, he told himself. The thought comforted him and he sighed once again. It was good to be home. He felt confident his parents would ultimately listen to him, as they had in the past.

A few moments later he remembered - Nani was waiting for him downstairs! He stretched out luxuriously once more, before he rose and returned to the sitting room downstairs. This was wonderful, too, with the cookies and the coffee waiting for him on the table, and dear grandmother hovering caringly around, fussing fondly over her grandson. Home, the pleasures of being pampered – Sandeep gave a happy sigh and relaxed comfortably on the sofa.

As she chatted to him of this and that it soon became obvious to Sandeep that his grandmother had not been informed about his choice of a life partner.

Well, she would know soon enough. Would she be as warm then, he wondered. He decided not to shock the old lady and wait instead until his parents returned. When he heard the click of the key at the front door he jumped up impatiently. "It is ok, Nani, go on with your coffee. I will open the door!" he told his grandmother, and rushed to the lobby to meet his parents.

"Sandeep?" queried his mother, surprised to see him there.

"When did *you* come?" asked his father.

As soon as Sandeep saw his parents indignant words tumbled out from his mouth, "I have to talk to you both! You cannot dismiss our feelings for each other so summarily...!" he cried, without wasting time over greetings.

"What is this? No hugs, no words to explain your sudden visit, and you are off on the same old topic?" scolded Gopal.

"I don't understand. Why are you so against them? I am not going to accept the ridiculous reason you give...!" Sandeep continued to argue, his voice growing more heated.

"Stop it, Sandeep!" It was his mother this time. "Is this the way you speak to your father? And better not mention it in front of your grandmother. She will be so shocked to hear that you... are... are... interested in that *chhokra's* daughter! It is just not right. Do stop talking about her, please!" She dismissed her son's protests and walked on to the sitting room.

"Don't bring up the topic before your Nani. OK? We will talk when we go upstairs," Gopal hissed a warning before he followed his wife to the other room.

The conversation remained stilted and forced as the family sat down to dinner. It was difficult to satisfy the old lady, who had a number of questions to ask about her grandson's unexpected visit. Nimisha warded off the queries by talking with great animation about her day at the office while Gopal remained just as vocal by describing his tiffs with colleagues at his work place. Sandeep sat in glum silence, broken with reluctant, distracted answers about his own activities.

If Mrs. Misra suspected that there was something strange about the behavior of the three diners around the table, she tactfully refrained from making any comments. The painful, awkward dinner was at last over and she retired to watch TV in her room, while the others climbed to their rooms upstairs.

"So you have come just to talk about that girl?" questioned Gopal, as soon as the three were alone.

"Stop calling her 'that girl', Dad. She has a name, Ursula, which is very charming. And as beautiful as she is! I respect her and love her!" Sandeep's voice was defiant.

"Please, stop arguing, beta. Yes, yes, we know she is a charming damsel, but you must understand why we object. She has grown up in the US and may well be cultured and educated, but how can we forget her background? We have told you - her father was just a *servant*. A '*chhokra*', just imagine! Someone uneducated, totally uncultured, capable only of doing the dirty work - the sweeping, washing, and cleaning - at someone else's home. He came from God knows which backward place in God knows which remote area. Think," she emphasized, making a face, "No education, no culture, no class, and, of course, though I do not like to say it - who knows which caste?"

"A low born untouchable, for all you know!" added Gopal with a snigger.

"Not that caste matters, of course," Nimisha remembered and warned her husband, realising that the word had no meaning for someone born in America.

"Well, that is true," replied Gopal, "But then, after all, we do belong to a much more respected caste... er... social class. You may not understand, Sandeep, but let me remind you, we are Brahmins, all said and done. How can we forget our ancestry? And that man ... could be a Dalit, a Harijan, or, anything ... your grandmother will be just too horrified when she learns. Don't ever mention it before her. "

Sandeep stared at his parents in shock. It was disgusting. How could they claim themselves as superior, just because they were born to different ancestors, a different family? And if Mr. Prasad had a job that included washing and cleaning, did it mean that he was an outcaste, an untouchable? He had always considered his parents to be modern and liberal, and could not believe that beneath that polished exterior were minds steeped in prejudice.

"Just imagine, what will your mother say when she realizes that her grandson wants to marry her ex-servant's daughter?" Gopal turned to enlist his wife's support to his objections, "It will be such a shock to the old lady. You know how class conscious the older generation is!"

"Much more than us! She will never tolerate such a situation! We live here in the US where things are different and there is more tolerance and equality. But for her, it is something never to be accepted!" Nimisha agreed wholeheartedly.

"No, never!" declared Gopal emphatically, "She is so proud of her lineage. How can she accept that man as part of her family?"

"But she liked Ursula!" burst out Sandeep, "She met her at Samir's wedding function. And she praised her. Not only that, she was happy when Ursula informed her about her father being in the hospitality business. She told me it was a good match. I am sure she will not object."

"She certainly will, when she realizes who the father actually is. She may have liked the girl but she will be totally shocked when she meets her father. Just as we were that day! She has always thought of that man, Ramua, as a servant, someone who can never, ever, be considered as our equal. And to have her grandson *marry* his daughter... Baap re! She can never, never agree to such a match!" Nimisha vehemently exclaimed.

"Totally out of question!" Gopal repeated the sentence once again, very emphatically. With these final words, he exited the room, leaving his son fuming with anger and disappointment.

"Pease, beta, don't make it so difficult for us. I know you are very upset just now, but such problems do occur when you are still young and immature. You will get over this soon and realize she is not really the girl for you," Nimisha tried to soothe her son.

"She is, she is!" Sandeep screamed in desperation even as his mother patted his shoulder and followed her husband out of the room. It was no use arguing with his parents, he concluded. They were just too stubborn. For a moment he wanted to run after them and resort to what he did as a child – throw a tantrum. Sometimes it did result in their giving way to his wishes, but often it did not, specially when his father had had a bad day at his office.

Sandeep thought about it but finally gave up the idea. It would only make them consider him immature, as his mother had commented earlier. It would be better if he stopped arguing and not confront them any longer.

He would think about it later and decide what he must do. However, there was no question about him changing his mind about the girl he would eventually marry. That decision was certainly not going to change, ever.

Chapter 30

A New Arrival

To Sandeep's relief and surprise it was Ursula who called him up before he could pick up the courage to do so. "I did not know your parents were such prejudiced guys. You cannot imagine how sad and shocked my father is. So is my mother. They told me I must try and forget you… there will be others who will accept me as I am," she said.

"My parents said the same to me!" replied Sandeep with a bitter laugh. This was followed by a tense pause over the phone.

"But we… cannot forget each other!" the words burst out at the same time from both. There was a long pause over the phone, broken finally by Ursula, "So let us meet!"

A relieved sigh escaped Sandeep's lips. "Yes, let us!"

Ursula took the initiative this time and hurried to her beloved's room as soon as her classes were over. When he heard the familiar, light footsteps, Sandeep rushed to throw the door open for her. The next moment the two were in each other's arms, kissing and embracing as if they had not seen each other for years.

"Alright, it is time to talk about what we must do now," Ursula separated herself from Sandeep's arms and said softly.

"My brother advised me to continue as before with you until I meet someone more suitable," complained Sandeep bitterly, "But I know there will never be anyone else for me."

"Nor for me!" cried Ursula, hugging him.

"We are each other's for ever and ever, isn't it?" murmured Sandeep tenderly.

"Mmm, yes," agreed Ursula snuggling closer and laying her head against his chest.

The two once again reassured each other about their love being eternal. Words not being enough, the reassurance progressed to passionate embrace, resulting in the two succumbing to urgent physical urges.

His work and her studies kept Sandeep and Ursula busy as the months rolled by, though they still managed to snatch precious moments of togetherness and pleasure whenever they could. The vexing problem of parental approval was pushed aside for the moment, postponed until they were both free to face it and find a solution. No harm in setting it aside; life was too full of other important issues. Why torture oneself with something that was beyond them to solve?

Nimisha called her son from time to time but stayed studiously away from any talk about the 'girl friend'. Sandeep was relieved. He did not bring up the subject either. Both his mother and he remained affectionate and courteous, careful not to stray into dangerous territory.

Irina, on the other hand, tried her best to warn her daughter to remain away from someone who was sure to forget her in the future. "Your father wants you to stay away from that boy. It is not going to lead you anywhere. If his parents do not want it, that boy is not going to marry you, he warns. Just remove him from your heart and mind. Concentrate on your studies instead. Believe me, he will not be yours, ever. Just forget him."

Ursula did not wish to get into any arguments with her mother, so she just mumbled, "Yes, Mom," and continued to do what her heart desired - meet Sandeep whenever she could.

It would have gone on this way for a long time had not Sandeep got an important call from his brother. "It has happened!" he heard the excited voice at the other end, "Pamela has just given me the greatest gift a wife could to her man! I have become a father! We are at the hospital just now with our little baby daughter. Come and meet her. She is the sweetest thing I ever saw!"

Sandeep was just as excited as his brother to hear the great news. He rushed to the hospital to meet his niece and felt thrilled to see the new arrival. He gazed in fascination at the infant lying in the crib, its tiny fists clutched against its body and its eyes tightly shut in a red, wrinkled face.

So this was what marriage had brought to his brother – a gift from heaven. It had enabled him to bring a precious human life into his world.

A sudden thought flashed across Sandeep's mind as his eyes lingered on the little infant. The union with his girl may also result in this. God forbid, if it happened before marriage by accident, would he be happy? No, certainly not! Neither would Ursula welcome such an arrival in their lives. What kind of life could the two provide for such a being, solely dependent on them for its future? Gingerly he touched the little face. Tiny eyes opened, the mouth yawned, a fist moved, before the wrinkled eyelids shut down again.

Thoughtfully, Sandeep gazed a while, his heart filled with a tender, protective feeling for the new- born just arrived into the world. "How do you feel?" he asked his brother.

"Overwhelmed by a sense of responsibility," replied Samir gravely, "Her future is in my hands. I hope I will give her a good life. So many other thoughts cross my mind. I am so glad I decided to marry Pamela. Suppose an accident had happened and, and....?" he shuddered and paused, "Hope you guys are careful? Your future is still uncertain, for you may, or may not - decide to marry! What will happen then?"

Sandeep nodded and fell into thought. His family was confident it was a passing phase and he was sure to get over it soon. Meanwhile, they probably felt, he was free to have a 'good time' with his current girl friend, as long as he was cautious and did not get into trouble. Well, he was certainly having a great time with Ursula, but contrary to what his family hoped, it was not something he would 'get over'.

Watching the expressions on his brother's face, of satisfaction mixed with pride, Sandeep realized that some day he too, would like to achieve the sense of fulfillment his brother seemed to feel. The warm glow of pride and joy that suffused his elder's face suddenly seemed to mock at him. 'You will never reach this stage! Yours is just a temporary bond, which will soon be broken!' his silence seemed to shout the words at him. It made him feel guilty, as if he was committing a sin by coming physically close to someone he could not make a partner for life. Deliberately he attempted to push aside the uncomfortable thoughts. He rose and said politely, "Congratulations for becoming a father," and added, "Are Mom and Dad coming to see her?"

"Yes. They are so excited to see their grandchild. Nani is also coming. She is just as thrilled as they are. In fact she wants to stay on with us to help with the baby, since Mom cannot, because of her work. But Nani has very kindly offered to stay here and look after the baby for us."

"Great. Sweet of her," replied Sandeep, "All the best for you, I must leave now."

So they were all coming here to welcome the new arrival. He would meet them all soon. Somehow the thought of meeting his parents did not make him as happy as it had done earlier whenever he met them after a gap.

Chapter 31

A Decision Made

The baby was soon home and a family get-together fixed to celebrate the new arrival. Sandeep decided to attend the party alone. There was no point in taking Ursula along, since she would not be welcome, as he well knew.

Amidst the music and the laughter he found himself sitting next to his grandmother. She was holding the precious bundle with the sleeping baby cozily ensconced in her lap. He felt her curious eyes fixed on him expectantly. "But where is your charming girl friend? I do not see her here. Isn't she invited? Are you two no longer friends?" she queried.

"Uh huh, she is busy, Nani," he muttered.

"Surely not so busy she could not spare an hour or two. She would have enjoyed all this," scolded Mrs. Mishra, spreading out her arms to include the roomful of guests, the music and the decorations, "Or, have you broken up with her?"

Sandeep did not know how to respond. He looked around for help, and met the eyes of his mother, who seemed to have heard the conversation. "Please come and help me, Sandeep. I need you here," she called out. Relieved, he quickly rose and followed his mother to the other end of the room. "Don't talk to your Nani about the girl," she warned him again, sternly, "I don't want to shock your grandmother. And by the way, are you still involved with her?"

Her words sent a wave of resentment and anger through Sandeep's heart. He controlled it somehow and managed to say in a low and firm voice, "I do not want to talk about it. You can think what you like. And now, it is time for me to leave. I'll just go and say goodbye to everyone."

To the surprise of the guests gathered there, Sandeep was the first to leave the party. Before he did so, he stopped near the baby's crib, where his grandmother had carefully tucked in the sleeping infant. His eyes were drawn once again towards the tiny face. How pretty and delicate she looked, clad in her pink, frilly dress, lying asleep in the midst of all the noise and activity. So helpless, so innocent! The warm gush of tenderness he felt for the little one flushed out the anger and resentment that had filled him earlier. He touched the baby's cheek, smiled at Pamela, his brother's wife, and bid goodbye a little more cheerfully before exiting.

All the way back home his mind continued to dwell on his predicament. He had made his decision already. Ursula it was to be. No other woman was going to rule his life and bear his children. Come what may, it would be her and no one else. Whatever his parents might say, he had definitely made up his mind. Would he break all ties with his family, if they refused to accept his choice?

Would he? He loved his parents; it was a bond, a strong bond between them, but ... his steps slowed down, his heartbeats quickened ... he loved Ursula and could not bear the idea of losing her. If it came to a toss between his parents and his beloved, whom would he choose? It was a heartbreaking thought, but he knew. Ursula, of course!

It was a foregone conclusion. Like with any youth about to set forth on the long journey of his life, it was the future that beckoned and decided his choices. His would-be mate, the companion who would hold his hand during the twists and turns of life was neither his mother, nor father nor grandmother, it was his beloved. The elders had played out their roles, guided him into adulthood, and now it was time for them to step aside and allow him to stride into the future with someone else he trusted.

By the time he reached home Sandeep had decided. He was not going to look for approval from anyone. He had made his choice and was going to stick to his decision.

Later, when he confidently told Ursula about his decision to go ahead and marry her when the time came, with or without parental approval, she looked shocked. "No, no, Sandeep. My people will not like it. My father was very particular about this. You cannot enter a home where you are not accepted, he told me. He advised me to forget you and to marry someone who welcomes me into the family."

"Then... why do you still see me?" asked Sandeep, puzzled at her objection.

"Because I love you. But I would certainly want your parents to accept me. I hoped, and still hope, that their objections would be forgotten. When they realize that we really cannot live without each other, they will accept me. That is what I would like; I would not want to marry without their acceptance... no, no! Please, Sandeep, please, make them like me, somehow! Otherwise, I don't know what my father would say!" she broke out passionately. Her eyes filled with tears and she hid them behind her palms.

Her reaction made Sandeep remember his grandmother's words. "Nani seemed to like you. Remember you met her that day? At Samir's wedding reception?"

"Yes. Sandeep, let us appeal to her, I am sure she will agree," suggested Ursula.

"No way!" protested Sandeep. "She is the one who objects the most. It was she who employed your father first, in India. She knows his background and will be shocked to hear that you are his daughter. Mom and Dad have warned me specifically – not to mention a word about your father!"

"I will appeal to her. Beg her to look at me and not at my father and his background. Surely she will like me as a person and not bother about my forefathers?" suggested Ursula.

"We... ell. We don't really know ... what she will do. I am not supposed to talk to her about all this, my parents have specifically warned me not to let her know. Let's not forget that," Sandeep reminded her.

"Hmm, let me think then... what can we do to make your people accept us? My father was so insistent. 'Only if they approve ...', he warned me. 'Otherwise I will find a suitable match for you and you will have to marry him', he said,' I will have to listen to him!" explained Ursula, her face lined deep with worry.

"You mean, he will force you?"

"That was his threat. Oh, Sandeep, do not let that happen, please!"

"Well, then there is only one solution. Just keep quiet and continue as before," concluded Sandeep, "And when the time comes, get married privately."

Ursula frowned. "No, no! We can't do that. My father is very old-fashioned. If he learns that we have been meeting each other, something I have kept hidden from him, he will really blow his top. Every time I come here I am so scared that he will find out. This has gone on long enough, Sandeep. It is only because of my strong desire to meet you again and again that we have gone on for so long. But it is turning me into a nervous wreck. How long can we continue like this?"

"I am so sorry. You did not let me know... I had no idea you were so nervous about meeting me... you hid it pretty well," remarked Sandeep.

"I had to. But it is time we did something about it, don't you think?" Ursula's voice was urgent and serious.

"Well, if you feel so strongly about it... we should. But what?"

There was no ready answer to his query and the two decided to sleep over it.

Sandeep's parents soon went back home to work and office. Mrs. Mishra, however, stayed back. "I'd rather be with a cute little gurgling baby than sit alone before a TV all day!" she remarked. This suited everyone because Pamela, too, looked forward to returning to work. And what better than to have a sweet old granny to take care of the infant and supervise the help's work! She could be at work the whole day, secure with the assurance that her baby was in loving hands. Her parents, confident that all was well and the new born in safe company, decided to return home, too.

Chapter 32

Dinner Invitation

Life for Sandeep continued as before. His work as a trainee at the Advertising Company kept him busy, though he was free to meet Ursula in the evenings. There were long gaps, however, between their meetings as Ursula, too, was busy with her final year studies.

It was Samir who rang up his brother some days later. "Hi dude, too busy to meet us? How is life? Can you spare an evening for us, too?"

"Sure," replied Sandeep, feeling embarrased. He had not bothered to visit his brother's home after the party at his place. "Will drop by sometime..."

"No, no, not *some* time, the coming Saturday evening! We plan to take Nani out for dinner. She has been such a dear. Helping with the baby and all. We must also do our duty. We want to take her out for a super Indian style dinner at some good Indian restaurant. How about that place we went to with your girl friend? Do you think it is a good idea? I know that restaurant belongs to Ursula's father. But the food was so authentic - she is bound to love it. We need not tell her who the owner is!"

Surprised, Sandeep did not respond for a while. What was wrong with Samir? Did he not know that his parents had warned him not to breathe a word about Ursula or Mr. Pershad before his grandmother? Why was he taking such a chance – suppose they met and she recognized him? And learnt about Ursula being his daughter?

"I know what you are thinking! Stop worrying. Mr. Prasad lives in New Jersey and is not likely to be at the New York branch. He was not there the last time we went there. No, no! It will be fine, let her enjoy that real Bihari dinner that we had that night. She is sure to love it! And maybe, we shall be able to find a way out of your present predicament. Have trust in your elder brother and God," Samir tried to reassure his worried sibling.

Reluctantly, Sandeep agreed to join his brother and his family at the Indian restaurant belonging to Ursula's father.

And then he got an invitation that left him speechless. "How is Ursula? Do bring her along! That is, if you both are still a twosome!" said Samir. The silence that followed his words made him ask, "Hey, are you still there, Sandeep?"

"Ye... es! But... are you sure? What about the objections made by Mom and Dad? They didn't want Nani to know anything about us. You know that, don't you?"

"I do. But Ursula is just your friend, not your fiancée. So it should be fine. You have every right to have a girl friend; you do not need to marry every girl you are friendly with!" laughed Samir.

Sandeep did not agree with his brother's assertion but was happy at the thought of an evening out with Ursula. "I will, then. Thanks. Hope Ursula is not too busy, and will join us for dinner. Thanks once again."

Ursula was delighted when she heard about the invitation. "Great! It will be exciting to meet your grandmother again. Charming lady. I quite liked her," she said.

"She seemed to like you, too. But I do not know what she will say when she learns about your father."

Ursula had a serious look on her face. It soon turned into a frown. "I don't understand why she should object, Sandeep", she said resentfully, "It is so unreasonable of her. My father is not the same person she knew long ago. You have seen our home and know how we live – as well as anyone else, if not better."

Without waiting for his reply, she turned around to leave. "Anyway, I must go now!" She said she had to hurry back since she had to present a paper at a students' meeting the next morning and needed to prepare for it. Before Sandeep could ask any more questions she had hurried out of the room. Though surprised at her sudden exit he decided not to worry about it.

Sandeep looked forward to the dinner. He had not eaten Indian food for a long time and realized that he had missed the mouth-watering dishes that a good cook could produce. Specially an Indian cook! He had been depending on his own casual eggs and bread cooking for too long. For change he had relied on the burgers and pizzas at the eating joint close by. They had removed his hunger pangs but were no substitute for the joys of spice - infused Indian meals.

Samir's invitation to a place where the food was sure to be most inviting made his mouth water.

Sandeep's emotions were a mixture of delighted anticipation and nervousness while he waited for the Saturday dinner. The thought of succulent, spicy and hot tandoori chicken battled with fear of all the questions his grandmother was bound to ask. Perhaps he should not take Ursula along. There was no knowing what she would blurt out once Nani shot her persistent queries and remarks at her.

However, he had already invited her and it would be awkward to tell her not to come. Sandeep worried about it as the day loomed closer and closer. At last he had made up his mind.

He would make an excuse and not take Ursula with him. Decision taken, he walked resolutely towards Ursula's dorm. There she was, strolling on the lawns with a friend. It was Angela, he found, when he drew closer. The two had not met for a long time and there were warm greetings between them.

"Angela has just given me some great news!" Ursula informed him excitedly as soon as she saw Sandeep. She hugged her friend and continued, "Guess what! Your old roommate Ben Maddock has proposed to her!"

Ben? Sandeep remembered his roommate, whom he had not met for a long time. After college their lives had led to different paths and he was not sure where he presently was.

Angela was quick to guess his thoughts. "He kept in touch with me, you see. He returned to his home in New

Jersey and found a good job there. We met each other from time to time and finally, last vacation, he came down to New York to spend some time with me. We became good friends until, last weekend, when he came here again, he took this step. He proposed formally to me! I am so happy!"

Sandeep congratulated her warmly. Ursula gave him a provocative glance, as if inviting him to do the same! He avoided looking at her. But he could not help asking Angela, "What about your future? Are you intending to settle down as a housewife after all that fiery talk about being a liberated woman?"

Angela laughed good-naturedly. "Being liberated does not mean I have to follow some great career. It also means that if I prefer being a wife and mother I am free to do so!"

"You mean take the easy way out and lead a lazy life, depending on someone else's hard work and income?" pointed out Sandeep with a smile that softened the harshness of his comment.

Angela did not take offense. "No! The work a housewife does is not any way less than what an office worker does. She needs to work just as hard, if not more, than anyone else. Do not underestimate the worth of a wife and a mother. That said, who says I cannot work once I am married? Of course I intend to pursue my career. Ben is sure to cooperate!"

"I am relieved to hear this. Your talents and education will not be wasted. Guess Ben and you have discussed this and he has agreed," Sandeep wanted to end the conversation but Angela was ready to chat further.

"I don't have to take his permission, Mister Wise Guy. It will be my decision - whether I wish to work at home or out in the world. And he is sure to agree to my wishes!"

Such confidence! Sandeep could not but admire Angela and her guts. He smiled at her and turned to Ursula. "Do you really wish to have dinner with my grandmother? I have been thinking - maybe it is not a good idea. She might ask all kind of questions and who knows what will happen if she discovers the truth...?"

"Come on, Sandeep! So what if she does? I will handle it, you need not worry!" Ursula interrupted to ask indignantly, "I am not ashamed of who my father is! I shall declare it proudly, even if she doesn't ask. I am not such a nervous goat as you seem to be!"

Angela jumped into the conversation to support her friend. "Three cheers for you Ursu! What is this, Sandeep? Why must she be nervous about meeting the old lady? How does it matter who her father was, or is? For you and for your family, it is only Ursula who matters! And you well know she is a fine person. People will be happy to welcome my friend into their family! Shame on you, I say! Shame, for doubting it!"

Sandeep could only stare at the two girls in surprise. They had expressed their feelings too strongly for him to counter their arguments. Quickly he backed off, only saying that it was fine with him as long as Ursula was prepared to face the consequences.

In fact, deep inside, he was glad to see that Ursula was prepared to face his grandmother, though she well knew there could be ugly, negative vibes from her.

Chapter 33

Ramu and his Worry

It was a pleasant evening in the Prasad home as husband and wife relaxed in the verandah overlooking the backyard. Spring had arrived. Greenery carpeted the ground, while the flowerbeds that bordered the lawn had little buds peeping out from amongst leafy plants. Tiny birds hopped around, chirping loudly and flitting around the leaves of the oak tree in the corner.

Irina was reading a book, while Ramu was deep in thought as he gazed at the garden. His eyes rested on the fresh greenery around him, but his thoughts were far away, centered on his recalcitrant daughter. He had just heard some news that had left him angry and disturbed. He had ordered Ursula not to meet that boy, but she had disobeyed him. According to the information received from someone he trusted, he had found that the two were still meeting each other, spending hours in each other's company. Like any conservative Indian father he felt outraged. How dare that boy meet his girl when his parents had rejected her! And worse, how could his daughter disregard his warnings, and his advice not to meet him, so blatantly?

Ramu's thoughts were interrupted suddenly by the shrill ringing of the mobile. Irina laid her book down and picked up the instrument. "Oh hello! Ursula? How are you?" She handed the phone to Ramu, "She wants to speak to you."

Ramu grabbed the phone from her and put it against his ear. "Ursula? Are you ok?" he asked.

"Yes, Dad. And you?"

"Fine. But what is this? They said you are still meeting that boy? Why? No! I said no! No meeting that boy! So why?" asked Ramu angrily.

"Yes, Dad. But you know I love him. So does he. How can we stop seeing each other?"

"But I told you... ," began Ramu indignantly, when she interrupted him quickly, "Please, Dad, don't ask me not to meet him! I will. I must. I cannot forget him."

Ramu frowned and handed the phone back to Irina. "Bad girl. She will not listen to her father," he told her, shaking his head in disgust. Leaving his wife to continue the conversation he strode out into the garden.

Irina's voice was gentle as she spoke to her daughter. "What is it, Ursu? What do you want? You will continue with him even when …?"

"Please don't ask me not to see Sandeep, Mom. I can't obey you in this. Please try to understand. Oh yes, and let me tell you, I have been invited to have dinner with the brothers!"

"Dinner? With whom, did you say?" questioned Irina, startled to hear the news.

"Sandeep and his brother! Samir is taking us all out for dinner. And you know where?"

"Where?"

"At Dad's restaurant in Queens! We had gone there once, long ago. They liked the food so much they want to go again! And he has invited me, too! Yes! After everything he still invites me! I am really thrilled!" Ursula sounded greatly excited at the thought.

"Well, that's a surprise, and you intend to go?" asked her mother.

"Yes, why not, when they have invited me?" replied Ursula.

"But I thought they did not want to have anything to do with our family!" asked Irina, puzzled.

"Well, Sandeep must have persuaded them. He loves me, Mom, don't forget. Just as much as I do! Well, anyway, why must I question them... I am happy to go!" said Ursula cheerfully.

"You know your father does not want you to meet him. Then why... ?" Irina asked in a stern voice but Ursula just laughed. She went on to talk about college and studies and managed to distract her mother from the subject.

"And you know, Mom, Sandeep's brother has become a father?" she chatted on happily, "he saw the baby. Looked so small and sweet, Sandeep told me. The whole family had come down to New York. Sandeep met them at the party given by his brother. His grandmother had also come. And, would you believe it, Sandeep said she was asking about me! She doesn't know, of course, about Dad. But she seems to like me, said Sandeep."

"Glad to hear. But wait till she learns about your father. The old lady may make things worse for you," warned Irina with a bitter laugh.

"Yes. But she has no idea, of course. She finds me good-looking, you know! Fair and all, thanks to you, of course!" Ursula gave a little giggle. "She knows I am a mix of Indian and American, which she doesn't seem to mind. I remember I also told her long ago that my father was in the hospitality business, which seemed to impress her. Ha, ha, she doesn't know any more than that!"

While the two continued with their lively conversation, Ramu roamed restlessly around in the back garden. Impatiently he pulled off the branch of a tree that had broken loose from its trunk, and strode to an empty corner, wondering if it would take root if he planted it there. A sudden thought made him halt. This was exactly how it was with his precious daughter; she too was breaking away from her parental roots. Would she be able to settle down happily in new surroundings? Well, that was life, he told himself. After all he had broken away from his roots too and planted himself far away in a distant land. And he had flourished there. Maybe his daughter, too, would be happy in her new life, in spite of the resistance she faced.

If only she had chosen someone more suitable than 'that boy'. Why did it happen to be someone from the same family he had run away from? Why, why? He walked up and down the tiled path that surrounded the grassy plot, his mind in turmoil. If only she had waited until he had found a suitable boy for her. There were many highly qualified young boys, both Indian and Amrikan, working with him. He knew them well. Any one of those boys would have made a good husband for his daughter. And of course, there must be other boys in her college who would have been just as good. But she had to choose someone absolutely unsuitable, someone whose family would perhaps never accept her. Why?

Ramu continued to stroll around listlessly in the garden with his disturbed thoughts to keep him company until Irina joined him at last. "So? What all did she say?" he asked her.

"Oh. Samir has had a baby girl, she told me. The whole family had come down to New York to see the little one," explained Irina shortly. "Come, let's go in. It is time for our dinner." She led him back into the house.

Later, when he was in a better mood, and as they lay closely and snugly together in bed, Irina spoke to her husband. "You were not nice to the poor girl. You were too short with her. She must have felt so bad about it. Let us not make her life worse by our attitude towards her," she told him.

"I feel bad also," complained Ramu, "Why she did not obey, when I said stop going to that boy?"

"It happens, love. You cannot help such things; you can fall in love with anyone. Did it not happen with us?" she gave him a tender smile, which immediately softened Ramu and made him feel better.

"You very good wife," he murmured.

"She is also a good daughter. We must not get angry with her. Let us think instead what we can do about this strange situation," suggested Irina.

Ramu nodded and clung closer to her. Indeed, he was lucky to have found a wife who could take away his worries and make him feel better.

Chapter 34

Best Indian Hotel

It was evening and time for dinner. Sandeep, accompanied by Ursula, arrived at almost the same moment, as did Samir with his grandmother and Pamela. They greeted each other outside the restaurant in front of a large yellow signboard that announced, "Best Indian Hotel," in shiny blue neon letters.

"Best?" exclaimed Mrs. Mishra, looking at the board with interest. She gave a little laugh. "Hope it turns out to be true!"

"I am sure you will find it good," Samir assured her and turned to his brother. "Hello, Sandeep! How are you, Ursula?" he welcomed him and his girl friend warmly. "Nani, this is Ursula, Sandeep's friend," he introduced her to his grandmother, forgetting that they had already met at his wedding.

"Yes, yes, I remember you, dear child. How are you?" the old lady nodded at Ursula, who bowed and greeted Mrs. Mishra Indian-style with a polite 'namaste'.

"As pretty as ever! Happy to meet you again!" Mrs. Mishra smiled back at her.

Samir, leading his grandmother by the arm, helped her up the few steps to the entrance. The little party made its way to an empty table in a corner of the hall and settled down around it.

"Nani, what would you like to have?" asked Samir.

"Anything you young people prefer. You are familiar with this place. I am sure you have your favorites. Go ahead and order what you like," replied his grandmother.

"Well, here are all the Mughlai dishes - curries, kebabs, biryanis," pointed out Sandeep, browsing through the menu card. "They have quite a variety. South Indian stuff like dossas are also available. In fact, food from around India - Gujerati, Kashmiri, Bengali - this place has it all. So... !"

"And from Bihar!" Ursula interrupted to point out, "Remember, we had 'litti chokha' - those stuffed puffy balls served with mashed brinjal and potatoes? It is something unique to this place."

"Oh yes, 'litti chokha'!" Sandeep shouted, trying to be heard above the din of the conversation around them. "Nani, would you like to have it?"

His grandmother nodded eagerly, "Yes, yes! Have not eaten it for a long time. In fact, since I left India. Imagine finding it here in the USA! How enterprising we Indians are! We have brought even this typical rural Bihari dish to America! I would love to try it."

"Sure, I will order it. What about the others? Hey, waiter, come and take our orders," Samir beckoned to the man who hovered around their table, waiting to note down the preferences of the guests.

The man recognized Ursula. He bowed to her, murmuring a welcome. She decided to ignore him and pointed towards Samir, "Ask him!"

The waiter turned to Samir, who placed his orders according to each person's taste. The guests, now that they were settled, had time to admire the place. Sandeep had noticed the colorful paintings on the walls earlier and now pointed them out to his grandmother. "Look at those murals, Nani! I really like them. They are so uniquely Indian."

Mrs. Mishra, her attention drawn to her surroundings, let her eyes wander with interest around the hall. She blinked in delighted recognition as her gaze fell on the walls. "Arre, but I know that style of painting! It is done on the mud walls of village homes in Jharkhand! For the Sohrai festival! How interesting! How did they come here?" she exclaimed in surprise.

Her grandsons, ignorant of the origin of the paintings, chose not to reply.

Mrs. Mishra was now listening to the melodious music that floated in the background. "That's a lovely Bhojpuri song!" she murmured happily.

By now Sandeep was very hungry. He had been looking forward impatiently to the meal. He eagerly sniffed the air and murmured, "Mmm, I can smell it already. Can't wait for the food to arrive. Good old Indian stuff!"

The air was indeed filled with the tempting smells of pure ghee being heated, of the frying of spices and the fragrance of cardamom and saffron that rose from the biryanis. He could feel his mouth water in anticipation.

Mrs. Mishra, who had been admiring the ambience of the place, turned now towards her grandsons. "I am so glad you thought of bringing us all here for dinner. I like this place. It is a welcome change for me. Your parents are so busy with their work and friends in Chicago that I often have to sit at home with only the TV for company."

"Glad you like it," said Samir, "You have been so helpful, looking after the baby for us. We had to do something, too!"

"And Sandeep, good you brought your friend!" Mrs. Misra glanced at Ursula, "Such a lovely girl! I am so glad to meet her again."

"Thank you," Ursula murmured shyly, "You are a sweet grandmother. I am happy we are meeting again."

"Yes, seeing you after a long time. We met at Samir's wedding. See, I have not forgotten you! That's because you stood out at the wedding. I wondered, who is that charming girl? Sandeep seems to have good taste, has chosen well! No wonder I did not forget!" Nani chatted on, while her grandsons looked at her in consternation. What would she say if she knew?

Fortunately the food arrived at last and the party settled down to enjoy their favorite dishes.

"Happy with your choice?" asked Samir lightly as he watched his grandmother break open the ball of baked dough filled with roasted gram powder, and pour warm ghee over the crisp crust. The ghee dripped down onto the gram powder that had spilled out of the 'litti'. She broke off a morsel, dipped it into the mashed brinjal -tomato- potato mixture and put it into her mouth.

"Good?" asked her two grandsons, watching her enjoy her meal.

"Mmmm... really tasty. Just the way I make it! It seems to have the special ingredients that I used when I made it in Delhi!" said Grandmother licking her fingers to savor the flavor of the ghee soaked gram powder.

"Isn't the food good, Nani?" added Sandeep enthusiastically, "The fish curry, too, tastes like the one you made the other day. Really scrumptious!"

"Oh, that's another dish from Bihar - fish in mustard sauce! It has mustard and garlic paste in a curry form. Your grandfather used to love it when I cooked it for him," Mrs. Misra remarked, her eyes turning misty as she remembered her late husband.

Another waiter was walking towards their table. He stopped near Ursula's chair and bowed, "Welcome back, Madam! You are here after a long time. Shall we get your special sweet dish for you, the one you had last time you came?" he asked.

"The 'makhana kheer'? Oh yes. That is one of the specialties of this place, isn't it?"

"Yes, Ma'am. And ... ," he tried to say something more, but Ursula cut him short. "You may go. Let us enjoy our dinner now!" she ordered before he could complete his sentence.

Sandeep caught his grandmother looking questioningly at Ursula. "Looks like you come here often. The waiter seemed to know you – what was he saying?" she asked.

Ursula flashed her charming smile at her. "Yes. I like the grub here, so I do come sometimes with my friends," she explained.

"Certainly worth it! It is so Indian and really authentic. Not like the fake Indian stuff cooked for the locals here, which is too mild for my taste. The spices too, are just right and in the correct proportion. No wonder this place is so popular," agreed Mrs. Misra. She glanced once again approvingly at the walls.

"So glad you like it!" Ursula replied.

"Come on, Nani, are you ready for the dessert? What would you like to have?" Sandeep pushed the menu card at his grandmother, trying to wean her attention away from Ursula and her familiarity with the place. Suitably distracted, Mrs. Mishra turned the pages of the menu. "I wonder if they have 'pua'... If so, I would love to try it," she muttered, "Oh, here it is, another specialty of the restaurant! Will you get it, please, Samir?" she turned to her host. Samir signaled to the waiter to place his order.

The man soon returned with Mrs. Mishra's choice. She helped herself to one of the fried sweet rounds, suffused with delicate flavours, and passed the plate with the rest around. "Let me see if this is as delightful..." she murmured. The next moment her eyes had lit up with joy. "Mmm, delicious! Again, just the way I make it, with fennel and cardamom! Perfect flavour!"

Sandeep had stopped paying attention to her. He had seen, from a corner of his eye, a couple entering the hall through the back door that led to the kitchen area. As the two stepped out of the dark into the better lit part of the hall he jumped up in shock and surprise.

The man, tall, slim and with a mop of white hair, looked smart in his black suit and blue tie. The lady who followed him wore a navy blue, formal dress. The two were clad in clothes different from what he had seen them in last, but he recognized them immediately.

To his shock he found that it was Mr. Pershad and his wife who had entered the room.

Chapter 35

The Meeting

As the couple drew closer Sandeep could not help wondering. How could a poor lad from a village, who had served his grandmother's household as a humble menial change so much over the years? If he had not known his past, he would surely have taken the man approaching them to be a successful businessman. The change was indeed something to be admired rather than condemned.

By now Ursula had also seen the couple. She sprang to her feet and rushed towards them. "Hey Mom, Dad, how are you here? When did you come?"

Sandeep saw his grandmother glance at the newcomers with curious eyes. "Oh, her parents? Is that what she said?"

Ursula had quickly steered the two away from their table. "Come, Dad. We'll sit there. Tell me - when did you come to New York?" Sandeep overheard her ask the elderly couple. He attempted to draw his grandmother's attention away from her. But the old lady had latched on to the words she had overheard. "Arre, she called him Dad!" she exclaimed, surprised, "So they **are** her parents? But why sit there, why not bring them over to meet us?"

"Maybe they want to talk privately! Come, let us enjoy our dinner, and let them be!" It was Samir's turn to divert Mrs. Mishra. Pamela, too, supported him by reminding them, "Oh! Isn't it time we returned? It is late and the baby may be missing her mother. We cannot leave her with the nanny for so long!"

Sandeep was dismayed to find his grandmother's eyes straying once again towards the table where Ursula sat with her parents. He wondered how and why those two had turned up there, on the very evening Samir had decided to take them for dinner at the restaurant. Was it deliberately planned? Who was to be blamed for this sudden, unexpected meeting?

"Pamela is right. We must leave now. Time to settle the bill," Samir agreed with his wife and raised a finger to signal the waiter.

"Just a minute, beta," Mrs. Mishra laid a hand on his arm to stop him. "I would like to meet Ursula's parents. Why does she not bring them here to meet us? Rather rude of her, isn't it? Call your friend here, Sandeep!" she ordered.

Her grandson looked helplessly back at her. He did not want his grandmother to meet Ursula's father and discover his earlier identity. But it was possible that she would not recognize the man at all. In that case, he could perhaps take a chance and allow the two to meet.

"Ask her to bring her parents here. I said I wanted to meet them," repeated Mrs. Mishra in the peremptory tone she used when she wanted to be obeyed. Reluctantly Sandeep walked over to the other table. He nodded his head to acknowledge her parent's presence before turning to Ursula. "She wants to meet them. Now what?" he whispered in her ears.

"OK. Don't worry. I'll handle it," she replied with a confidence he was far from feeling himself. "Come, let me introduce you to Sandeep's family," she told her elders.

"Sure! But who is that lady?" asked Irina.

"I am sure Dad knows!" replied Ursula, glancing at her father.

Mr. Prasad merely nodded and gave no reply. He looked uneasy, as if he did not like what he saw. Irina, however, rose with a confident air and he followed her, awkward and stumbling, obviously nervous about meeting those on the other table. As soon as they reached Ursula announced, "Meet Mr. Pershad, the owner of this grand, successful restaurant, and my dear father. And this is my darling mother!"

"Such a surprise! But very happy to meet you!" smiled Mrs. Mishra, "Do sit down. Oh, so you are the owner of this place? I am really impressed. The food here is just great. I enjoyed the dinner so much."

So she had not recognized him? Sandeep let out a deep sigh of relief. Perhaps it was because the lights were dim, or was it because she was seeing him after a gap of several years? During that long period, he had perhaps changed beyond recognition. Or maybe her eyes were not sharp enough any longer. After all she had advanced in years. Whatever the reason, he was happy to find that there were no signs of any recognition on her part.

"So glad you liked the meal!" Irina was the one who replied. Her husband, who no doubt had recognized the old lady, looked down dumbly at the floor. "My husband worked really hard to maintain the high standard of cooking at his restaurant. He taught his employees how to make those special Indian dishes. He supervised the cooking himself until he was sure that they had learnt it well, down to the last ingredient."

Sandeep kept his fingers crossed and hoped the conversation ended soon so they could all leave the place. His grandmother, however, was obviously enjoying the conversation. "It is not just the food, it is the overall ambience of the place. I like the music and the decorations on the walls, and everything else around here. I believe your husband owns other such eating houses, too," she said admiringly to Irina.

"Oh yes! We have other restaurants in the US that serve Indian food," agreed Irina proudly.

"And what about those paintings? Who did those?" was the next probing question from Mrs. Mishra.

"Oh, those? Tell her," Irina urged her husband, who had not yet raised his eyes from the carpet at his feet.

"What! Paintings?" startled, Mr. Prasad stammered, "Sh... she did. Urmi, girl from my village! I knew her well. She came ... showed paintings in London. Paris also. Then in New York. She had big exhibition here. I saw exhibition of paintings at Museum. I said, come to my hotel, do my walls, so she came and painted here. Good, no?"

"Very," agreed Mrs. Mishra, "In Bihar we have Madhubani, but in Jharkhand it is a different style and is called Sohrai. I have read about it, so I know. Imagine seeing it here! How did she agree to do the walls at your place? Did it cost you a lot?" she asked inquisitively.

"No, no, told you, she was my friend. I know her, from my village. Good friend, Urmi was! Became big, famous artist. Her daughter is also Sohrai artist. The husband was no artist, but he knows about art and he made her great," replied Mr. Prasad.

"Good for her!" smiled Mrs. Mishra. She was staring now at the gentleman in black with a puzzled frown on her forehead. Suddenly she leaned forward, her eyes narrowed and focused on Mr. Prasad's face. "Excuse me, but your wife said that you were the one who taught your people how to cook Indian food. I am curious about the Bihari dishes. The 'litti chokha', the fish curry and the 'pua' were so perfect. Just the way I cook that special stuff. Did you teach those dishes to your staff?"

"Yes," mumbled Mr. Prasad. He looked at his wife, then at his daughter, and then hung his head down again.

"And where did you learn them from?" Mrs. Mishra asked eagerly, sharply.

At last Mr. Prasad raised his head. But his eyes evaded hers and darted from one face to another, as if at a loss and hoping to be rescued. She, however, continued to stare steadily at him. The frown on her forehead had deepened and she shook her head as if still unsure.

"But how is it possible?" she spoke at last in a puzzled voice, "You cannot be the same person. How can it be?"

A hesitant smile now hovered over Mr. Prasad's lips. The others waited with baited breath.

"The same ingredients... the little bit that I added to make the 'pua' special... it was my idea, to add to its flavour... how?" she asked. "**HOW?**" she repeated, her voice sharper and aggressive now. She pointed her finger accusingly at the man before her. "How is it possible, I say, unless... , yes, you are the very same person!"

Sandeep knew that she had recognized Mr. Prasad at last.

Chapter 36

Mrs. Mishra and Ramu

Ramu bowed his head, and looked too nervous to say anything. Irina's eyes reflected her shock and embarrassment. She too was totally at a loss for words.

Ursula was the first to react. "He is my dear, darling Dad!" she cried, as if that explained everything. She laid a protective hand on her father's arm.

Her words were greeted by complete silence from those seated around the table. The music in the background, too, had fallen mute, as if to allow the astonished group to voice its feelings.

Mrs. Mishra glared at father and daughter and exclaimed, "Ramu! Of course! I should have understood. You are Ramua! And you are the girl's father!"

Still no one spoke, waiting for further response from the old lady. It was Ursula again who broke the tense silence. "Yes. He is my father. And this is Irina, my Mom. Dad, you have already met Sandeep and his elder brother. This is Pamela, his brother's wife, and ...", she paused and pointed at Mrs. Mishra, "This is their grandmother. Dad, you recognize her, don't you? Yes. She is the one who turned you into a skilled cook. She is the person who brought you all the way here to the USA. You are grateful to her, aren't you, as you told me once years ago? If she had not brought you here, you would never have become the rich owner of a chain of restaurants serving Indian food! Isn't that so, Dad?" she spoke breathlessly fast, trying to break the awkward silence that had fallen over the group.

Mrs. Mishra was still staring at Ramu and shaking her head in disbelief. "So it is you, Ramu. Such a shock to me! You are Ramu, no, Ramua! Unbelievable. Mr. Prasad, Ursula's father, is none other than the old Ramua I knew," she repeated the words to herself, to the continued discomfort of her listeners.

"Ji, Ma'm!" Now that his identity had been revealed to the old lady, Ramu seemed to relax. He raised his head and looked directly into his old employer's eyes. He rose and, hands folded in greeting, stepped boldly towards her. "Yes. I am Ramu, Ma'am. Namaste, Ma'am." He bent down to touch her feet in the Indian gesture of respect for the older person.

It was not so easy to please his imperious 'memsaheb'. She shook her head in disapproval and showed her refusal to accept the humble greetings by hastily withdrawing her feet away from him. Ramu's hands missed the respected feet by several inches. He drew back to stand stiff and awkward before her.

"But it was very wrong of you to have run away, Ramu. Why did you do it?" Mrs. Mishra addressed the culprit in an aggressive, accusing tone.

"I got a good offer. Could not say no...," mumbled her old servant.

"You could have told us. It was very wrong of you – you just sneaked away! Like a thief, without telling anyone! After we had done so much for you, brought you all the way here...!"

"For your own benefit, of course," muttered Irina resentfully. Her voice was low, but it reached Sandeep's ears.

"Come on, Nani," he urged his grandmother, "No need to scold him now! He did what he had to do – and surely you will agree that it turned out well. Look at what he succeeded in doing – establishing so many Indian restaurants for people like you, who miss real Indian cooking!"

"Well, that may be true," Mrs. Mishra reluctantly conceded but continued indignantly, "That does not make up for what he did. Surely he could have accomplished it in a better manner. Explained what he wanted to do, taken permission... been more decent about leaving us."

"Ok, let me ask you to forgive and forget," Irina butted in, trying to be reasonable. "I know you are good people. That is why, when I learnt from Ursula that Sandeep's brother had invited her for dinner here, I told my husband we must go and meet the two young men and the girls. We did not know, of course, that you would be here, too. We were so surprised to see you. But now that we have met, let me tell you. We, too, are a respectable family. Let us talk and get to know each other. We are so fortunate that Sandeep's grandmother too happens to be here. Now let us forget the past, please. Let us all try to understand and be friends with each other, shall we?"

Ursula stepped forward to declare, "May I add... my Dad has risen from a poor lad to someone equal to anyone!" she forcefully asserted. "You must appreciate that. You cannot treat him now as if he is still a humble servant! No! And you can't look down on us as people socially below you."

Samir did not like his grandmother to be told off thus. "Come on, let's leave, Nani. I am sorry you had to go through this. We should not have brought you here. Sandeep, get up! I know Mummy is going to be angry with us for bringing Nani here."

"It is alright," protested Sandeep, "Ursula and her parents are just trying to explain things. No need to get so upset!"

"We are not saying anything that is wrong," Ursula added, "I am just defending my father. He is not someone to be looked down upon, as your family seems to do! He may have been a poor guy once, but now he has reached a very different level. I would like to tell your grandmother that those old-fashioned distinctions of caste and class no longer apply, in any case. We are all the same, and equal! Old people must learn to accept this!"

Pamela, listening quietly all this while, decided to join the conversation, "Samir, we don't have to leave. Mrs. Prasad is right. Maybe we should talk things over... what do you think, Naniji?"

The old lady, looking tired and visibly disturbed by the arguments thrown at her, sighed and leaned back in her seat. "Will everyone sit down, please? Let us not create a scene in front of all these people," she glanced at the other diners in the hall, many of who had turned around to stare at them. "Ramu, you may take a chair. Sit down. Let us talk like civilized people. No need for everyone to get so agitated."

Ramu still held back humbly. Irina and Ursula propelled him forward and pushed him into a seat just next to Mrs. Mishra. She shrank aside a little, as if to distance herself from her old servant. Soon she regained her composure and straightened herself until her shoulder just touched the other's sleeve. She looked around and smiled faintly, trying to assure her grandchildren that it was fine with her.

Suddenly the music struck up, with a sweet voice singing a melodious song that proclaimed all to be one happy family. It made Sandeep raise his hands and laugh. "Sweet song! Just listen to it everybody! Let us all agree to what it says! What do you think, Nani?" He had to shout to be heard. But heads began to nod in time to the rhythmic beat, and lips stayed shut, for no conversation was possible.

Mrs. Mishra closed her eyes, as if to snatch a few moments of peace, though the music playing in the background was not so soft. The conversation seemed to have stressed out the old lady. A few minutes later, however, Sandeep saw her swaying to the infectious beats of the song.

"None is high, none low, before Him we all bow!"

The words of the song rang out clearly as it echoed and resounded repeatedly across the hall.

"None is high, none low, all hold hands and bow!"

The music became faster and louder, drowning all other sounds in the hall. Mrs. Mishra's eyes were still tightly shut. She seemed to be listening closely, concentrating on the words that echoed persistently in their ears.

"None is high, none low, before Him we all bow.

Up into the sky we go, to be welcomed equally.

For, He created us as one big family,

Let's remember, the sky belongs to all,

Before Him, we are just one big family!

None is high, none low, all hold hands and bow!"

Sandeep waited for the song to end. He watched his grandmother begin slowly to nod to the music. Her body seemed to gradually unwind, her tightly closed fists opened and her fingers relaxed to stretch out on the white tablecloth.

Mrs. Mishra had remembered her husband. Her mind went back, back, to that time years and years ago, when she had asked him, "Is it alright to make that boy cook our food? After all, we don't know what he is, for I never asked – what is his origin, I mean. And we are - you know what! Should we...?"

Before she could complete her question he had interrupted her, "Come on, you cannot discriminate between people like that! We are all the same! A human being is just that! Equal to any another born on our earth. You know I do not believe in the division of society into superior and inferior beings!"

And so she had gone ahead and turned the 'chhokra' into a cook, remembered Mrs. Mishra with a wry smile.

How would Mr. Mishra have reacted in this situation? Watching them from his world up there in the sky, where he now belonged, and where he was now closer to the heavenly beings present there, would he have changed?

The words of the song came back to her. No. On the other hand, he would have believed even more strongly in it. The song only confirmed it further. "None is high, none low, before Him we all bow," the words echoed loud in her ears.

None was less equal, or superior to the other. That was what her dear husband had believed.

And that is what he would repeat today too - that just as the sky was the same for all, those on earth, too, ultimately, were all one.

As soon as the song was over, Mrs. Mishra's eyes flew open. She glanced at the anxious faces around her and gave a long, deep sigh as if she was letting go not only of the shock and anger that she had felt on encountering her former employee, but also of the old prejudices that had shackled her generation. Her expression was now calmer as her gaze shifted to Ramu, humble, his head bowed, a nervous twitch on his lips. She gave another sigh, and smiled at them apologetically. There was a more cheerful expression in her eyes, which seemed to lighten the wrinkles on her aged face.

It was Ramu whom Mrs. Misra addressed when she finally spoke, in a voice that was no longer aggressive "Well, Ramu, I must say you have come a long way. I well remember the poor, miserable lad who stood at my door that day, seeking a job. You were ready to do anything- sweeping, cleaning, and all the dirty work! But I am glad I taught you other skills as well, and turned you into a good cook. You picked up so fast. To think that you have now turned into a great hotelier! What a surprise! I am so happy that you made the most of it! You certainly deserve to be congratulated for turning into a successful entrepreneur, instead of attending to others and carrying out their orders all your life. I feel proud of you."

"Thank you, Ma'am!" Irina breathed out in relief. Her voice was gentle, her eyes moist.

Ramu did not say a word, just folded his hands once again and bent towards Mrs. Mishra's feet. "No, no, Mr. Ram Lakhan Prasad! You are as much a gentleman as I am a lady! Yes, we are all the same! No highs and lows!" she smiled, giving a sideways glance at Ursula to see how she reacted. The girl nodded and smiled in agreement, though her eyes had become large with the tears that had quickly welled up in them.

"Bless you, child, you are as sweet as you are lovely!" cried Mrs. Mishra, opening out her arms towards the girl. Ursula ran close, and was caught in a warm hug by the older woman.

Sandeep turned to his brother, a question in his eyes. Samir patted his shoulder, smiled and muttered, "It's ok, dude. I don't think our parents are going to object any more. Congratulations!"

Sandeep's face was a picture of relief and joy. He exchanged a glance with Ursula that expressed more than any words could have done.

There was no further talk as the music struck up again, playing a rumbustious, romantic Hindi film song this time. Feet began to tap to its beat. Nani lifted her hands to clap in time to the fast rhythm.

"I love you, you love me, love makes us all free! That's why a happy, happy family are we!" the singer's deep voice rang out, and the walls echoed the words all around the hall.

Soon the youngsters on Sandeep's table had sprung to their feet. Both brothers, along with their girls, scrambled towards the dance floor and were soon dancing away in gay abandon.

Ramu looked on gravely with great pride at his family and at his surroundings. His eyes were filled with tears of happiness. His daughter had been accepted. This was the best and the final proof - of the fact that he had at last reached where he had always wanted to. It was really true – that the great, big, sky, filled with dazzling stars, was within reach of all who were born down on the earth below.

Mrs. Mishra gazed affectionately at them all. Her hands clapped and her feet tapped enthusiastically. She looked at her family, its members laughing and enjoying themselves. There was Sandeep, his arm around his girl, smiling at her.

Samir and Pamela danced together, hand in hand. She felt satisfied, proud that she had made them happy by accepting the newcomers into the family.

Yes, her husband was right. In her heart Mrs. Mishra thanked him for giving her the right message at the right time.